FAMIL

in the

NORTH YORKSHIRE DALES

Howard Beck

HIGH INTEREST · LOW MILEAGE

Scarthin Books, Cromford, Derbyshire   1992

FAMILY WALKS
in the NORTH YORKSHIRE DALES

Family Walks Series
General Editor: Norman Taylor

THE COUNTRY CODE

Guard against all risk of fire
Fasten all gates
Keep dogs under proper control
Keep to paths across farm land
Avoid damaging fences, hedges and walls
Leave no litter
Safeguard water supplies
Make no unnecessary noise
Protect wildlife, wild plants and trees
Go carefully along country roads
Respect the life of the countryside

Published 1992.

Phototypesetting, printing by Higham Press Ltd., Shirland, Derbyshire

ISBN 0 907758 52 5.

MILL GILL FORCE   Route 9

Preface

Whichever way one views the Yorkshire Dales it is walking country par excellence, the very epitome of England's green and pleasant land. It matters little whether the visitor seeks historical links with the landscape or prefers striding along the wind-swept 'tops' to a more sedate amble along the meandering, tree fringed rivers of the verdant valleys; it's all here, an infinity of contrasts simply awaiting to seduce the unprepared and guarantee that interest never wanes.

The region covered by this guide is centred upon that area of the Yorkshire Dales to the north-east and east of the Three Peaks region, dealt with in my first Family Walks guide. The area is contained more or less within an imaginary triangle linking Richmond with Grassington and Kirkby Stephen.

Some of the walks pass through little known valleys, others explore more familiar terrain. At all times the countryside is dramatic and sometimes unexpected, sweeping dales and wild moorland edges offering expansive panoramas. There are sad ruins from the heyday of lead mining, Norman castles, earthworks and Bronze Age circles, sleepy stone-built villages and picturesque waterfalls secreted away in wooded gills and gorges.

~~~~~~~~

About the author

Howard Beck works as a freelance photographer and writer of guides and books. His work has featured in many local and national publications, such as The Lady, Field, The Illustrated London News, Country Walking, Yorkshire Life, Police Journal, Country, Climber and Rambler and Dalesman.

He has contributed the Three Peaks and Malham, and West Yorkshire titles to Scarthin Books Family Walks series.

His other books include:

> GAPING GILL, 150 Years of Exploration (Hale).
> BRONTE COUNTRY [joint photographer] (Trodd Pub.).
> FAMILY WALKS AROUND SKIPTON (Dalesman).
> WORDSWORTH COUNTRY (under consideration).
> CAVES OF THE CLOUD FORESTS (in preparation).

CONTENTS

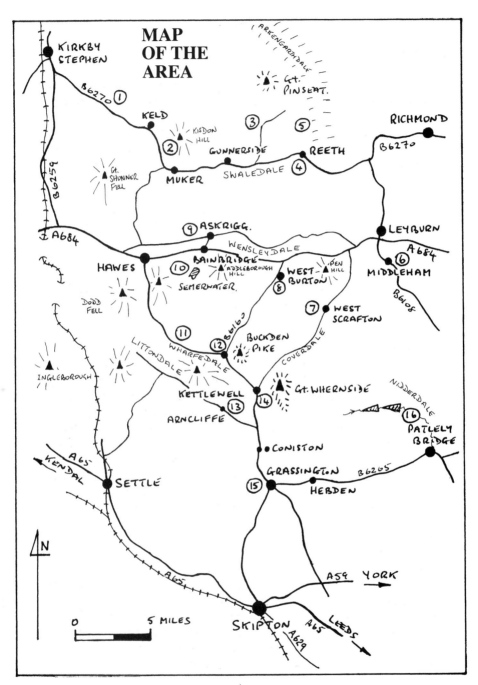

MAP
OF THE
AREA

KIRKBY STEPHEN

B6270 ①

KELD

ARKENGARTHDALE

Gt. PINSEAT.

③

⑤

RICHMOND

B6270

② KISDON HILL

GUNNERSIDE

REETH

Gt. SHUNNER FELL

MUKER

SWALEDALE

④

⑨ ASKRIGG.

LEYBURN

WENSLEYDALE

A684

HAWES

⑩ BAINBRIDGE

ADDLEBOROUGH HILL

WEST BURTON

PEN HILL

⑥ MIDDLEHAM

B6108

SEMERWATER

⑧

DODD FELL

⑦ WEST SCRAFTON

INGLEBOROUGH

⑪

WHARFEDALE

LITTONDALE

B6160

⑫

BUCKDEN PIKE

COVERDALE

Gt. WHERNSIDE

NIDDERDALE

KETTLEWELL

⑬

⑭

⑯ PATLEY BRIDGE

ARNCLIFFE

CONISTON

KENDAL

A65

GRASSINGTON

B6265

SETTLE

⑮

HEBDEN

N

A65

A59 YORK

0   5 MILES

SKIPTON

LEEDS

A65

A629

4

Introduction

Choosing a walk

Unless children in the party are seasoned ramblers it is perhaps advisable to select easier routes initially, moving on to more sustained expeditions at a later date. In the Appendix at the end of the book an attempt has been made to grade the walks in terms of difficulty. The reader may find this of value in choosing suitable walks that avoid placing too great a demand on younger children too soon in their walking life. The aim is to nurture interest rather than put the child off walking for life!

Allowing sufficient time

Many of the walks will form the best part of a day's outing, at a child's pace, allowing time off for play, exploration and rest stops, whilst for some walks a half day will suffice. It is infinitely better to over-estimate rather than under-estimate the time required; there is nothing worse than having to route march the last stages of the journey. As a rough guideline, allow a pace of around one mile per hour for very young children, graduating to two miles an hour for, say the more experienced ten-year old.

What to wear

The British weather being what it is demands that walkers go prepared for the worst. Robust, but comfortable fell shoes or walking boots are more desirable than wellingtons, even though the latter have their place in English folk heritage! They do tend to chafe on long walks. Waterproof outer garments are an essential rather than a luxury, while underneath, several layers of thin woollies are far better than one thick jumper. They tend to be warmer when the conditions are cold and in hotter weather (we do get it warm now and again) allow greater flexibility. Don't forget a woolly hat and gloves. A strong rucksack is essential for carrying spare clothing, food, drink, maps and so on.

Finding the way

Most of the walking described is along well defined and marked public footpaths, bridleways, green lanes and with the occasional stretch of road where this is unavoidable. Though each of the route descriptions and maps should be sufficiently detailed for navigation it is recommended that the relevant Ordnance Survey sheet is taken along as well. Should the reader find a path obstructed then the line of least resistance around it should be sought and the problem reported either to the Ramblers' Association or to the relevant District Council.

Refreshments

Where stated pubs along these walks allow children on the premises if accompanied by an adult. Many cater for young children with the inclusion of play areas or special rooms. Bar meals and lunches are usually available but a good alternative, and one which will go down well with the younger walker, is to take along a picnic. Places on route where this is ideal are mentioned, as are the locations of cafes and tea shops.

Public transport

Although these days most families possess a car or other means of transport, I have included relevant details of bus operators, trains, etc. in the Appendices.

LIMEKILN, BIRKDALE

KISDON FORCE   Route 1

Symbols used on the route maps

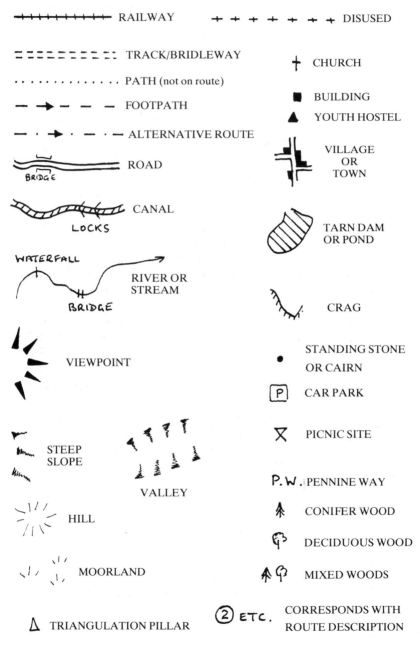

++++++++++ RAILWAY

+ + + + + + + DISUSED

= = = = = = = :: TRACK/BRIDLEWAY

. . . . PATH (not on route)

— ➤ — — — FOOTPATH

— · ➤ · — · — ALTERNATIVE ROUTE

ROAD
BRIDGE

CANAL
LOCKS

WATERFALL
RIVER OR STREAM
BRIDGE

VIEWPOINT

STEEP SLOPE

VALLEY

HILL

MOORLAND

△ TRIANGULATION PILLAR

† CHURCH

■ BUILDING

▲ YOUTH HOSTEL

VILLAGE OR TOWN

TARN DAM OR POND

CRAG

• STANDING STONE OR CAIRN

P CAR PARK

X PICNIC SITE

P.W. PENNINE WAY

CONIFER WOOD

DECIDUOUS WOOD

MIXED WOODS

② ETC. CORRESPONDS WITH ROUTE DESCRIPTION

8

Route 1

(shorter variation 3½ miles)

Five Dales Walk

Outline   High Bridge ~ Ravenseat ~ Carrack Force ~ East Stonesdale ~ Keld ~ Kisdon Force ~ Angram ~ High Bridge.

Summary   This is a superb introduction to the Dales landscape and the way the geology has influenced its final appearance. It offers both long and shorter versions touching on five dales in one of the most beautiful and unspoilt corners of the north. Well signposted on good pathways.

Attractions   The upper reaches of the Swale valley, centred upon Kisdon Hill, is one of the finest and certainly most dramatic areas in the Yorkshire Dales. From its source at the Birkdale watershed, Birkdale Beck is joined by Great Sleddale Beck to become the infant River Swale.

Within three miles it is augmented by streams flowing south from three smaller valleys, Whitsundale, West Stonesdale and East Stonesdale, before flowing off through the Kisdon Gorge. The main attraction of this route has to be its many cataracts, eight named ones altogether.

Combined with its waterfall scenery, the sweep of the moors, its woods and idyllic dales makes this a most memorable outing. The walk starts where Birkdale and Whitsundale merge to become Swaledale. Field paths are followed north into Whitsundale, returning down dale by way of the dramatic canyon at How Edge Scar and the strangely named feature, Oven Mouth.

Back once more in Swaledale an easy retreat to the start is possible, but in not continuing on to Keld the best features of this walk would be missed. Keld village is little more than a hamlet but is situated at the heart of countryside moulded by the forces of nature.

Here the Swale has carved itself an impressive gorge along the northern flank of Kisdon Hill. Ten minutes stroll downhill from the hamlet is East Gill Force and further down river, the dramatic Kisdon Force. Stark white limestone bluffs contrast with the native ash and oak woodlands.

From Keld a path climbs the side of Kisdon Hill briefly tracing the Pennine Way and the famous Swaledale Corpse Way. It passes through the hamlet of Angram for the exposed moors, returning to the start at High Bridge in Birkdale.

Refreshments   Park Lodge tea garden, Keld (summer only).

Route 1

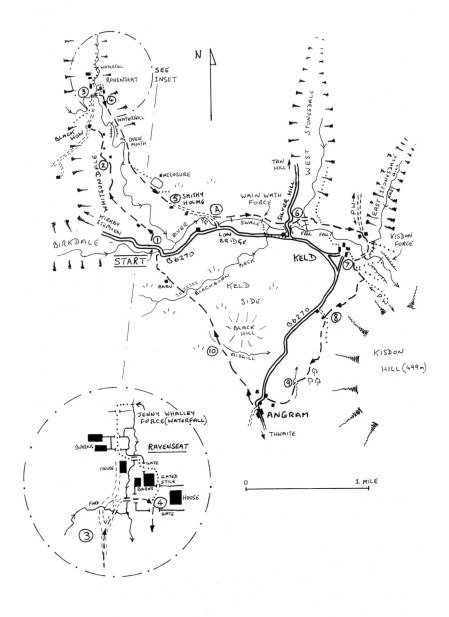

Route 1

Five Dales Walk

7 miles
(shorter variation 3½ miles)

START *High Bridge (G.R. NY871014) where the A6270 crosses Birkdale Beck 1½ miles west of Keld. There is space to park just off the road west of the bridge. O.S. Outdoor Leisure Map 30 (Wensleydale sheet).*

ROUTE

1. *Leaving the car, cross the stile opposite and walk uphill to the stile in the top right corner of the pasture. Cross the stile, then forward between wall and a barn. At the next corner, cross a stile and, with wall on your right, head for a gate.*

2. *Through the gate bear diagonally right, for a stream and across a stile left of the next barn. Turn right along the wall, then right again through a stile beyond ruined barn. Turn left and follow the wall to Black How House. Turn right along road into Ravenseat.*

3. *Cross two bridges, bearing right through a gate into a yard in front of a house. Turn left through a stile and left beyond barn. Go through a gate and over a footbridge, tracing the wall around to the right. Go through three gates then turn right to a waterfall. Return to the yard in front of the house.*

4. *Go through a gate along a south-trending path. This divides beyond Oven Mouth. Take the right branch, passing an enclosure, to another parting. Go right (**signed Keld**) to Smithy Holme Farm.*

5. *Turn left down the track and at the trees veer left uphill through a wall gap. Continue on path following edge of Cotterby Scar to the road at Silver Hill.*

6. *Turn right then left through a gate along the track to East Stonesdale Farm. On the right just before a bridge is Carrack Force. Continue on the track for ½ mile, joining the Pennine Way at the farm. Follow it to the right, between buildings, and down towards East Gill Force (**picnic spot**). Turn right crossing bridge over the river, and right again uphill to a gate. Go through this and shortly meet a path at right angles.*

7. *A right turn leads into Keld and gives access to Catrake Force. Turning left however, reaches a gate, then a fingerpost (**signed Kisdon Force**). To see the falls turn left along a rocky trail to the riverside. Returning to the sign, turn left and soon meet another signpost. Ignore this and, in a few yards, scramble to your right up the edge of a low scar. Turn sharp right along its brink tracing the path uphill to a sheepfold and a gate.*

11

Ignore this, instead walking up the wall side through a gap, then on a path descending by a barn to a bridleway at the foot of the hill.

8. *Turn left uphill to a gate. Go through this and veer immediately downhill, on a vague path through gorse leading to a wall. Walk left along this, but before a corner turn right through a gate. With the wall on your left descend to a stile. Cross this and walk below wood to meet a wall, and follow this left to a corner. Cross a stile and turn right to wall, then left along this over a footbridge to a gate.*

9. *Go through gate and at the top left corner of field go through a gap. Walking uphill with wall on your left, meet the road and turn left. Go right at a phone box. Just beyond this turn right through a stile and ascend by a limekiln to a gate. Go through this, climbing to a wall gap, then along wall to a corner. An obvious path continues forward and left to Aisgill.*

10. *Cross the stream and left along wall to cross a stile. Turn left on obvious path over moors to Blackburn Beck. Ford the stream to a track (**not on map**), then continue along a green rake amid heather. Cross a stile to the right of a barn, then forward crossing two more stiles. Turn right and walk down wall side to High Bridge.*

SHORTER VARIATION

As for 1 to 5 above then:

A. *Descend to and cross Low Bridge and turn right along the B6270 to reach the starting point after ½ mile.*

ACCESS BY BUS

Being a circular walk one could start at Keld to which United Buses run service No. 30 from Richmond.

Route 2

Kisdon Gorge and Muker

Outline   Muker ~ Kisdon Hill ~ East Gill Force ~ Kisdon Gorge ~ Ivelet Wood ~ Rampsholme Bridge ~ Muker.

Summary   A classic circuit starting and finishing in Muker village. The route crosses Kisdon Hill down to the Kisdon Gorge near Keld with its waterfall scenery before returning down river. The walk has an initial steep start out of Muker to join the Pennine Way where a shorter option returns via Thwaite and meadowland. The route follows well marked paths and bridleways throughout. Throughout the walk there are spots ideal for picnics, play stops and stick dipping or paddling; in short, a fine day.

Attractions   Muker is a picturesque village, especially when approached from the west or north. It has a Literary Institute of unusual design and a church. Prior to 1580 however, the deceased in the upper valley had to be interned at Grinton, the nearest consecrated ground. They were carried down dale in wicker baskets along a route followed known today as the Corpse Road, a route which can still be traced.

It is exciting countryside where the sound of rushing and falling waters is never very far away. To my mind Swaledale is one of the loveliest valleys, famous both for its hardy black-faced sheep and of course the many field barns.

This walk has an initial steep start climbing out of Muker to join the Pennine Way where it comes up out of Thwaite. The shorter option takes off at this point descending toward Thwaite.

Thwaite is a tiny cluster of stone-built cottages, forming a settlement that grew up within a clearing in a former forest. Its name derives from the Nordic tongue meaning a forest clearing.

Thwaite is famous as the birthplace of the Kearton brothers, Cherry and Richard, who were pioneers in the study of nature and wildlife photography, with which they illustrated a number of books.

Crossing Kisdon Hill from the south on the approach to Keld enjoys views toward Rogans Seat and Swinnergill over to your right. From Keld village access can be gained to Catrake Force, another impressive cataract formed where the aggressive power of the river has cut down the riverbed.

continued on page 16

13

Route 2

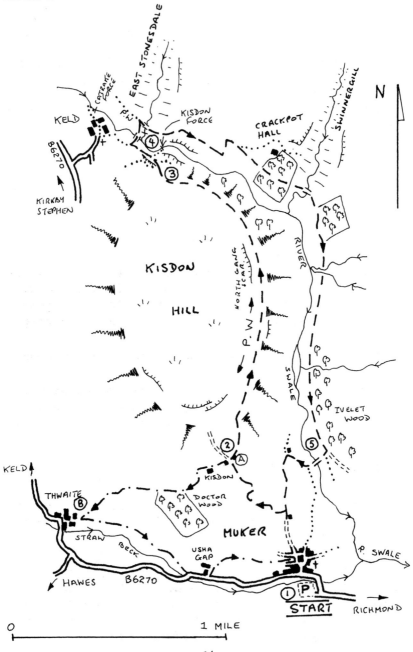

East Stonesdale

Cotterby Force

Kisdon Force

Crackpot Hall

Swinnergill

P.W.

KELD

B6270

KIRKBY STEPHEN

(4)

(3)

N

KISDON

HILL

NORTH GANG SCAR

RIVER

P.W.

SWALE

IVELET WOOD

(2)

(A)

KISDON

DOCTOR WOOD

(5)

KELD

THWAITE

(B)

STRAW BECK

USHA GAP

MUKER

P. SWALE

HAWES

B6270

(1) (P)

START

RICHMOND

0   1 MILE

Route 2

Kisdon Gorge and Muker

5 miles

(shorter variation 2 miles)

START *Muker village is reached from Hawes via the pass of the Buttertubs, or along the B6270 (Kirkby Stephen 12 miles; Richmond 21 miles. A car park is provided by the bridge at the eastern end of the village. (G.R. SD911979) O.S. Outdoor Leisure Map 30 (Wensleydale sheet).*

ROUTE

1. *Walk into the village and turn right after the Literary Institute. With post office on your right continue forward along a lane (**signposted Keld**), climbing uphill to a gate. Go through this and ascend the track to a junction by a barn.*

2. *Leave the bridleway and go right, still climbing, then contour around the hillside by North Gang Scar.*

3. *Descend to a fingerpost beneath a crag. A right turn here leads to Kisdon Force, but going straight on for a short distance, a right turn with the Pennine Way leads down to the river. Cross the bridge and, with East Gill on your right, walk uphill to join bridleway. Turn right over the bridge and go through gate.*

4. *Follow the track east, crossing Swinner Gill and passing several woods to a junction at Ivelet Wood, adjacent to a bridge.*

5. *Turn right across the bridge. Ignore the path going left, to proceed right along the river towards a barn. Turn left on a path to the far right corner of a field. Here, a walled lane is followed to a gate. Go through this and trace the outward bound route back into Muker.*

SHORTER VARIATION

As for 1 to 2 above then:

A. *Bear left and go through a gate. Follow the Pennine Way (**yellow waymarks**) to Kisdon Farm. With this on your left continue forward and left down to Doctor Wood.*
   Bear right above the trees and descend a stony path towards Thwaite.

B. *Immediately before entering the village, turn left along an obvious field path (**signposted Muker**), tracing this to the B6270. Turn left, then left (**signpost**) at Usha Gap Farm. Pick up a stile to the right of the house and go through this, heading for a gate. Go through this, then with a wall on your right follow field paths back into Muker.*

On the northern side of Kisdon Hill the Swale has cut itself a deep gorge flanked by limestone cliffs. In these wooded depths Kisdon Force leaps noisily into deep plunge pools.

A steep continuation from Keld passes through woods to a footbridge where the Swale has its confluence with East Gill. The latter falls majestically down three steps, an idyllic spot suitable for picnics and play.

Behind East Gill Force a bridleway crosses a bridge spanning the beck. This forms part of the coast to coast long distance path linking St. Bees Head with Robin Hoods Bay. Following this gives easy going through several small broadleaf woods where one may spy a variety of bird species, tree creeper, nuthatch, wren and woodpecker.

At Rampsholme Bridge the Swale is crossed again and Muker regained by way of a narrow leafy lane adjacent to riverside meadows that are a riot of colour in early summer.

Refreshments   Farmer's Arms Pub (tables outside) and Old School Tea Rooms in Muker, Park Lodge tea garden in Keld (summer only). Kearton Guest House Tea Shop, Thwaite.

OLD GANG MILL

Route 3   5 miles
Hard Level Gill

Outline Surrender Bridge ~ Old Gang Mill ~ Brandy Bottle Incline ~ Flincher Gill ~ Forefield Rake ~ Great Pinseat ~ Surrender Bridge.

Summary This fine walk, although passing through some wild country is not difficult, following good tracks all of the way. There are some interesting mine ruins on route and excellent moorland scenery offering distant views from the high point of the walk.

Attractions Swaledale was one of the great leadmining areas of The Dales between the 17th and 18th centuries. At Old Gang and nearby Gunnerside Gill some well preserved mine buildings stand as time-enduring testimonials to all the hardy souls that toiled below ground seven days a week.

Slightly downstream from Surrender Bridge is the remains of the Surrender Smelting mill where galena (lead sulphide) was roasted to reduce it into the metallic lead required for industry. To reach the temperatures required needed a good draught. Behind the mill the line of the flue can be seen climbing Barras End to where the chimney once stood.

From Surrender Bridge a former mine road, now a public bridleway, traces the east bank of Old Gang Beck almost a mile, as far as the Old Gang Smelt Mill. Here the well preserved ruins include the chimney of the pre-roasting oven, hearths, dressing floors and the flue, seen trailing up the hillside behind. Above too are the surviving pillars of the peat store where fuel was kept for the roasters. The mill ceased working in 1885.

Opposite Old Gang Mill a large spoil heap marks the entrance to an abandoned mine level. Beyond the mill the stream becomes Hard Level Gill, a name reflecting the trials of lead mining. Soon a track branches left over a bridge. Just ahead is Level House, a former miners' lodge.

The valley then narrows with the great scar of Northrake Hush over on your left. A hush was a method of shallow ore extraction. A dam was built on high ground above a vein. When the head of water was released the force tore up the ground along the vein carrying the ore with it. The great depth of some hushes is the result of repeating the process many times.

Some 600 yards beyond Level House can be seen Brandy Bottle Incline on the right, now blocked but once providing access to Hard Level, one of the most productive lead mines in Swaledale.

continued on page 20

Route 3

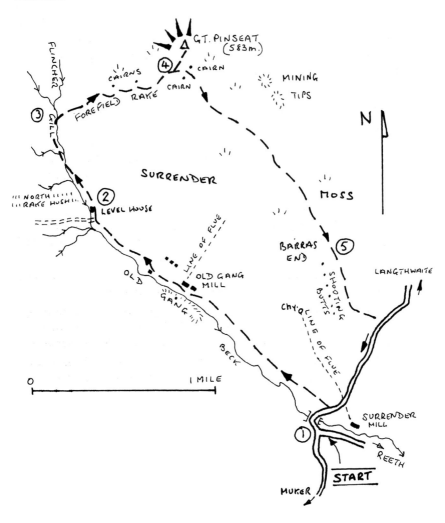

Route 3

Hard Level Gill

5 miles

START   *Park at Surrender Bridge (G.R. SD989999) on the Langthwaite to Feetham moor road a mile north of the latter. O.S. Outdoor Leisure Map (sheet 30 Wensleydale).*

ROUTE

1. *From the bridge walk up the road a few yards in the direction of Langthwaite, then turn left along a track (**signposted bridleway**). Follow this to the Old Gang Mill a mile distant. Beyond the mill the track climbs briefly where a stream emerges. Shortly the track divides by a settling pond. Ignore a left branch, and walk uphill, then continue as far as Level House Bridge.*

2. *Do not cross the bridge, but continue ahead following the right bank of Flincher Gill. After fording the beck go uphill and join a track from the left, turning right here. Continue beside a line of bell pits to a second ford 200 yards ahead. Cross the stream and go through a gate.*

3. *Proceed uphill through mine tips (**route marked by cairns**). At the head of Forefield Rake two cairns are reached on spoil heaps.*

4. *Turn left here across the moor toward the fell wall 150 yards away, behind which is the triangulation pillar at Great Pinseat. Return to the twin cairns and continue south on obvious path across Surrender Moss.*

5. *At Barras End the track descends with a line of shooting butts over on your right. At the road turn right and follow this back to the start.*

Via Forefield Rake the route turns east for the summit of Great Pinseat. Although the top lacks character, on a clear day the view extends across the head of Arkengarthdale and beyond to Bowes Moor and the Stainmore Gap.

Turning south from Pinseat two miles of often boggy going crosses Surrender Moss where, if one believes local legend, followers of Bonnie Prince Charlie surrendered.

The moor road is reached and just before the starting point at Surrender Bridge the road crosses the line of the flue climbing the hill from the smelt mill.

Refreshments   There is nowhere for refreshments on route, so perhaps best to carry your own.

FOLK MUSEUM, REETH

Route 4   4½ miles

Reeth and the Maiden Castle

Outline Reeth ~ River Swale ~ Maiden Castle ~ Grinton ~ Swaledale Folk Museum ~ Reeth.

Summary Starting in Reeth pleasant stretches of the riverside path lead eventually to the open moors and the Iron Age fort at Maiden Castle. Descending back to the valley level, a bridleway returns through meadows to the start via the village of Grinton and a museum. This route offers easy going on good paths with no undue difficulties. The walk is well route marked and ideal for the whole family.

Attractions Reeth may rightly be referred to as the capital of upper Swaledale. It is a magnificent village with its cottages, shops, cafes and several public houses forming the perimeter of a huge green.

Should the weather prove less than kind there are two craft shops, a pottery and an excellent folk museum where exhibits feature local life, industry and costumes.

From the village a ginnell and path lead down to a suspension bridge spanning the Swale. Upstream from here the route passes through riverside meadowland which in early summer is vibrant with colour. Flowers that may be seen on route include vetch, meadow cranesbill, harebell, campion, birds-foot trefoil and early purple orchid. There are several places where picnics could be taken and opportunities to look out for dippers, flycatchers and (if you are up early enough) herons and kingfishers.

Leaving the riverside for the open moor the route takes in the Maiden Castle, a fortified earthwork probably dating from the Iron Age when Venutius was rallying the Brigantes against the might of Rome in A.D. 79.

A return to the river is followed by an easy bridleway leading to Grinton with its ancient church and neat cottages. Parts of the church are Norman, including the bowl of the font. The return to Reeth from here is via Arkle Beck and the museum.

Refreshments Kings Arms Pub (children welcome) and Copper Kettle tea rooms in Reeth. Bridge Hotel (outside tables) in Grinton. Alternatively why not take a picnic and have it by the idyllic riverside?

Route 4

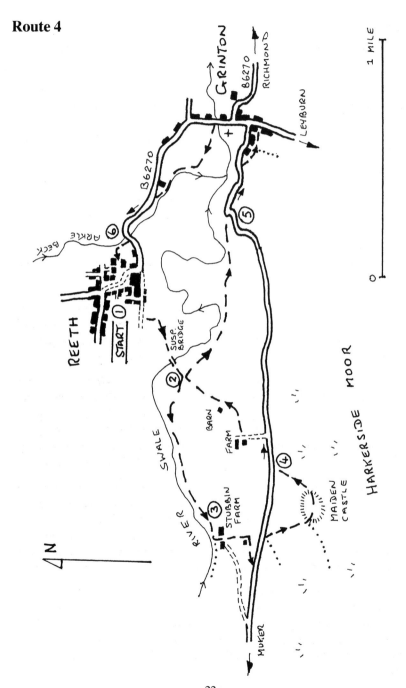

Route 4

Reeth and the Maiden Castle   4½ miles

START *Reeth (G.R. SE039993) is easily reached by car from Darlington (A1 and A6108 to Richmond then B6270 26 miles) or Northallerton (A684 to Leyburn, A6108 and B6270 35 miles) O.S. Outdoor Leisure Map 30 (Wensleydale sheet). There is plenty of car parking space around the village green.*

ROUTE

1. *From the Kings Arms walk south between Barclays Bank and White House Crafts. Turn right on a path (**signposted to the river**). At the road turn left then right at 'T' junction. Follow the lane to a gate beyond Quaker Garth then turn left down a path to a gate by some barns. Go through this, down wallside, then right at the signpost (**Grinton**) to the river bridge.*

2. *Cross the bridge and walk straight forward to a gate left of a row of thorn trees. Ignore this, instead walking along fence to a corner and turning right. Follow bridleway to a corner and go through a gate on your right (**sign**) along a path to the riverbank. Turn left.*

3. *After ¾ mile ascend left by a wall to a corner. Turn left through a gate and walk through Stubbin Farm. Go forward uphill, through a gate near a barn, and turn right to reach the moor road. Turn left along the road to the second bridleway (**signposted Castle Bolton**). Take the path climbing towards a tree on the skyline. Walk east along the banking of the Maiden Castle, then follow a vague path back down to the road.*

4. *Turn right, then left into the first farm. Turn right in the yard, go through the first gate (**yellow paint spot**), following a track. Leave this before the next farm to veer left through a gate (**yellow spot**). From a power line pole head for a gate 50 yards right of a farm. Go through gate and continue downhill. Turn right on a bridleway before the river bridge, following obvious route for ¾ mile to the road at Swale Hall.*

5. *Turn left, then right at a bend through gap stile (**signpost**), then left immediately over a second stile. Walk along the bottom of the field through two more stiles, then go diagonally left, through a gate. Pass between the houses and turn left into Grinton. Cross the river bridge and turn sharp left at first stile, tracing field path for ½ miles to the B6270. Turn left.*

6. *Cross Reeth Bridge and turn sharp left through a stile (***signed Beckside Walk***). Double back beneath the bridge across a stile and turning right. Go through a gate after 120 yards and follow path uphill to a gate, and steeply from there between buildings back into Reeth, passing the museum on route.*

ACCESS BY BUS
United Buses service 30 from Richmond and Darlington.

EMERGENCY SUPPLIES?

Route 5

7¼ miles
(shorter variation 3¼ miles)

Arkengarthdale

Outline Arkle Town ~ Langthwaite ~ Scar House ~ Booze ~ Strothwaite Hall ~ Fremington Edge ~ Castle Farm ~ Arkle Beck ~ Arkel Town.

Summary Arkengarthdale forms a superb setting for this walk, a little longer than some in this guide and perhaps best reserved for the more experienced family group. It is hard going in places, with some steep sections, but always on good well-marked paths. The views from Fremington Edge are well worth the effort however.

Attractions Arkengarthdale is the long and not so well known valley through which the unclassified road passes from Reeth to Tan Hill on the Durham border. It is a wild dale with only two villages of any size. Like Swaledale, into which it is a tributary, this dale has in the past seen a great deal of lead mining.

Evidence of T'owd Man's activities, the ubiquitous tips and ruined buildings, have with time been assimilated into the surroundings, so that today they seem as much a part of the natural landscape as do the miles of dry-stone walls.

Arkle Town where this walk begins is little more than a hamlet formed of a few cottages; Langthwaite on the other hand is a fully-fledged village, complete with pub and church. The arched bridge leading across Arkle beck into Langthwaite may be recognised by those who enjoyed watching the T.V. series All Creatures Great and Small.

After a riverbank route from Arkle Town has passed Langthwaite a climb by Scar House leads to footpaths downdale to Booze, a hamlet funnily enough without a public house! A descent to Strothwaite Hall then precedes a steep climb up through a mined region to an airy stroll along Fremington Edge. The views from here extend eastwards to the Hambleton Hills.

Back in the valley once again, along field paths and the riverside, the route returns to the start at Arkle Town to complete a very enjoyable circuit. Although there are plenty of places for scrambling and play **do not allow children near disused mine working and shafts.**

Refreshments Red Lion Inn (tables outside). Children welcome.

25

Route 5

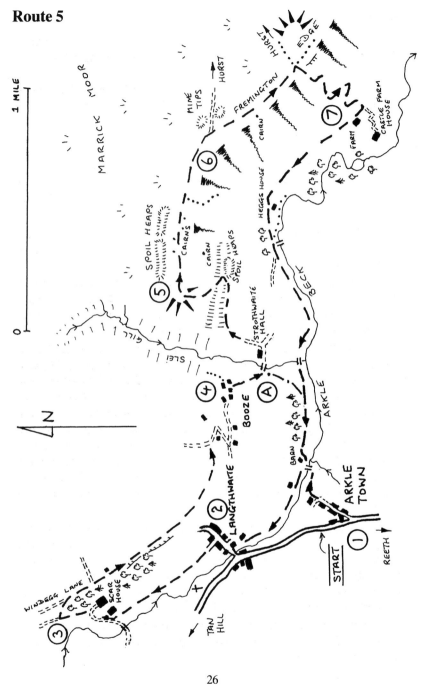

Route 5

Arkengarthdale

7¼ miles

(shorter variation 3¾ miles)

START   *At Arkle Town located on the Tan Hill to Reeth road, 2½ miles from the latter. Parking beside road at (G.R. NZ008019) O.S. Outdoor Leisure Map 30 (Wensleydale sheet).*

ROUTE

1. *From the junction at Arkle Town walk down lane beside Calver View to where it bends left. Walk straight forward through a stile (**sign**), going through old burial ground, then downhill to the river. Cross bridge and turn left to reach Langthwaite.*

2. *Turn right into village, then left to face the pub. Turn right past the village store, then left in front of Ellers House, on track to a gate (**yellow spot**). Obvious field path passing a ruined barn continues to Scar House. Head for a gate to the left of the left-hand building, then with house to your right walk down to tarmac drive (**bridleway**). Turn right. Where it bends right into courtyard, turn left up dirt track through trees and go through gate. Continue forward beside wall.*

3. *Just before the track levels turn right, cross a stile (**blue paint**) and climb towards the top of the wood and a gate beyond. Go through this, turn right along a green lane and forward (**signposted Fremington**) to a gate by an old farmhouse. Go through gate. Where the path dips bear left, climbing to a fence. Walk along this, cross a stile and continue on a vague path along the scarp edge (**care**). Path becomes more obvious to a stile. Cross this and, climbing beside a fence, cut across an enclosure, beyond which another stile is crossed. Where the walls meet go through the right-hand gap, then veer right along the base of a small spoil heap. With a wall on your left a bridleway is reached and traced right, down to a lane.*

4. *Turn left toward Booze, through a gate at Town Farm. Turn right between a shed and a barn to a gate. Go through this and a second gate. Field path descends to a bridge over Slei Gill. Cross this and turn sharp left (**signed Hurst**) immediately after Strothwaite Hall. Climb (**blue paint spots**) to a gate. Go through this and turn right, soon passing through mine tips and winding left to Fell End after ¾ mile.*

5. *Turn right (**route not clear but cairned**) through the mining fields with a large cairn in front and to your right. The Bridleway soon becomes clear and heads for a wall corner.*

6. *Go through a gate and walk along Fremington Edge, with a wall on your right, passing some bell pits and cairns. After ½ mile a path joins from the left. Turn right across a stile and walk forward (**path is vague**). At the dale edge a clear route zig-zags down to Castle Farm.*

7. *Turn right in front of gate, and follow bridleway behind the farm, continuing to a gate above Heggs House. Go through this and follow wall down to the left, through a gate. Bear right behind house, then down farm track to signpost (**Reeth**). Turn right and follow riverside for ¾ mile to the footbridge below Arkle Town. Cross bridge and climb uphill back to the start of the walk.*

SHORTER VARIATION

As for 1 to 4 then:

A. *Ignore the bridge across to Strothwaite Hall, instead turning right down a track through woods to join riverside path back to the bridge over Arkle Beck. Turn left over this and climb uphill back to start of walk.*

THE SWINE CROSS, MIDDLEHAM

Route 6

Middleham and Coverham Abbey

Outline   Middleham ~ Low Moor ~ Tupgill ~ Coverham Abbey ~ Hello Bridge ~ Cover Banks ~ William's Hill ~ Castle ~ Middleham.

Summary   For anyone interested in the history of The Dales this walk is a must. The route follows excellent paths and bridleways, offering easy walking throughout, with plenty of features to interest children and parents alike. Riverside sections contrast with field paths and woodland, taking in a Norman motte and bailey fortification, a castle and abbey ruins.

Attractions   Middleham's magnificent castle is located on the south side of the town. This was the childhood home of King Richard III and has one of the largest keeps ever built. This reflects the importance attached to Middleham as a seat of power in the 15th century.

Middleham also has a long tradition of racehorse breeding, established originally by the monks at Jervaulx. This will no doubt interest Dad if he is one for the occasional flutter on the races.

The site is now managed by English Heritage, and amongst displays that may be seen is a replica of the now famous Middleham Jewel, a 15th century gold and gem pendant found in nearby fields in 1985.

Some 500 yards to the south-west is William's Hill, site of a Norman motte and bailey fortification. Here children will no doubt enjoy playing 'king of the castle'. This was built soon after the Conquest by Ribald, brother of Alan the Red of Richmond, to safeguard his estates and secure a road which came over the fells from neighbouring Coverdale.

The timber and earth fortification was abandoned when the new castle was built in the late 11th century. Middleham is a fine example of a Dales market town with handsome Georgian residences and a number of public houses either side of its square.

At the west end of town is the so-called Swine Cross, built to mark the granting, in 1479, of a fair and market by Richard, Duke of Gloucester, later King Richard III. The cross represents the weathered likeness of a pig, believed by some to be the white boar emblem of Richard.

Middleham also has a long tradition of racehorse breeding, established originally by the monks at Jervaulx. This will no doubt interest Dad if he is one for the occasional flutter on the races.

Leaving town by way of the castle the route strikes out across Low Moor. On almost any weekend horses may be seen being exercised here. Two miles west from the start the route turns south through stud farms and stables at Tupgill and returns along the river Cover via the haunting ruins of Coverham Abbey.

Route 6

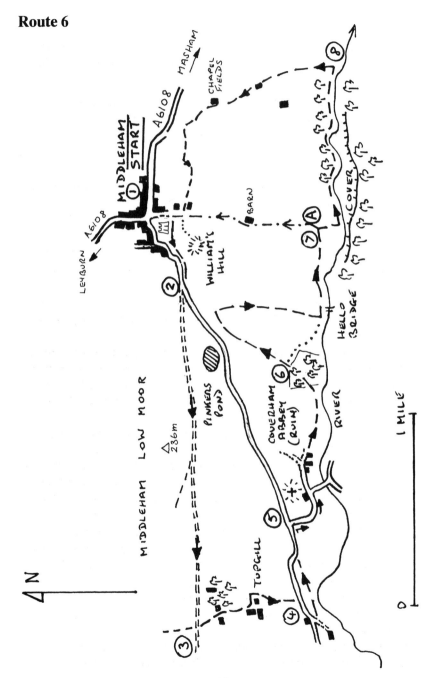

30

Route 6

Middleham and Coverham Abbey

6½ miles

(shorter variation 5¾ miles)

START   *Middleham (G.R. SE128878). The town is easily reached from Ripon by the A6108 to Leyburn and is 2 miles from the latter. O.S. Outdoor Leisure Map 30 (Wensleydale sheet).*

ROUTE

1. *From the square walk past the Black Swan, turning left immediately after. Continue forward on a track with castle on your right to a stile. Turn right and follow field path, crossing two more stiles, then with wall on your right proceed to road.*

2. *Cross road to a gate. Go through this, turning left to follow a bridleway west across Low Moor with Pen Hill seen in front. After 2 miles bear left to a wall side and follow this right to reach a tarmac track.*

3. *Turn left through the gate into Tupgill Park, following the track downhill between stables. Turn left at the clock tower, then first right and continue downhill to the valley road.*

4. *Turn right then left toward Bird Ridding Farm. 30 yards ahead, turn left (**signed Coverham**). Follow a path with the river down to your right to reach a gate. Go through this and continue along a fence, then across pasture to a stile near a water trough. Cross stile and turn left, fording a stream, then turning right along the road.*

5. *At the junction go right (**to Caldbergh and W. Scrafton**) downhill to river bridge. Ignore this to walk straight ahead beneath arch and past Coverham Nurseries. Take right fork after Garth Cottage, and go through the gate. With a farm on your right follow a track past shed to a gate. Bear left through this to second gate then, after a ruined building, climb uphill past a barn and through a small wood to a stile.*

6. *Cross this and walk uphill to road, then double back downhill to Hello Bridge. Ignore this, instead crossing the stile to the left, following a path climbing Cover Banks. Aim for the top left edge of a stand of pines, cross two stiles and turn right along a fence (**yellow arrow**). After ¼ mile cut across the field (**green arrow on fence**) to a wall.*

7. *Turn right down wall side to a stile. Turn left across this and along riverside path for ¾ mile, ignoring a left branch beyond a broken wall. Cross a ladder stile into the woods, down banking and over another stile. Ignore next gate to continue beside river (**look for yellow arrows**).*

8. *Cross stile where trees end and turn left over the hill, through a gate into Straight Lane. Continue along track and, soon after Chapel Fields, cross a stile on the left. Trace field path forward, then left uphill to a stile. Cross this and, with football field on the right, go through a stile to the left of the next gate. Walk between hedges to a gate and turn right back into Middleham.*

SHORTER VARIATION
As for 1 to 7 then:

A. *Turn left up wall and, just after barn, go through a gate. With wall on your left walk over the hill and down to gate. Go through this and along track passing the castle back into town.*

ACCESS BY BUS
United Buses service 159 from Richmond (infrequent).

———————

Refreshments   Black Swan pub (beer garden at rear) and White Swan (outside tables). Nosebag and Castle Keep tea shops, all in Middleham.

MIDDLEHAM CASTLE

Route 7

Coverdale

Outline   West Scrafton ~ Caygill Bridge ~ Carlton ~ Gammersgill ~ Turnbeck Lane ~ Nathwaite Bridge ~ West Scrafton.

Summary   An easy half day outing taking in two villages having Anglo-Saxon roots. The route follows footpaths, green lanes or bridleways and is generally easy, though it does have a short steep climb at both ends.

Attractions   West Scrafton is an unusual village, unusual in the sense that not very far beneath its unassuming cottages lie the ramifications of Scrafton Pot, a cave system discovered by potholers in 1967.

Having explored this cavern personally I can vouch for the fact that some parts of it come uncomfortably close to the surface. One day some poor unsuspecting soul, with their feet up in the living room might suddenly disappear in a rumble and cloud of dust!

In Caygill at the point where the beck sinks it is interesting to note how some cottages cling perilously close to the brink of the shattered cliffs.

Both Carlton and West Scrafton were mentioned in the Domesday Book, the latter having been passed on to Ribald at the time of the Conquest, when it was said to be 4 leagues long and ½ wide. Before 1066 it was valued at 10s. The name Scrafton is reputed to mean the 'town by a hollow in the ground'.

Coverdale is a pleasantly quiet dale which seems to have escaped the crowds usually associated with more popular regions of the National Park. It is sandwiched between Colsterdale and Walden, overlooked by the high ground of Little Whernside and Dead Mans Hill to the south, its northern flank rising to Penhill, where a tumulus is said by tradition to be the last resting place of a Celtic chieftain.

The walking is very pleasant, leaving Scrafton alongside the impressive Caygill Scar, before crossing the river Cover and climbing to Carlton. This is probably one of the longest villages in the Dales. Mel Beck plays cat and mouse along the main street, in places culverted, elsewhere being exposed in picturesque stretches coloured with clumps of marsh marigolds.

Passing the Foresters Arms to the western extremity of the village we see Platts Farm, above the entrance of which is a tablet commemorating the life of Henry Constentine, the Coverdale Bard, a locally celebrated poet who died in 1869.

continued on page 36

33

Route 7

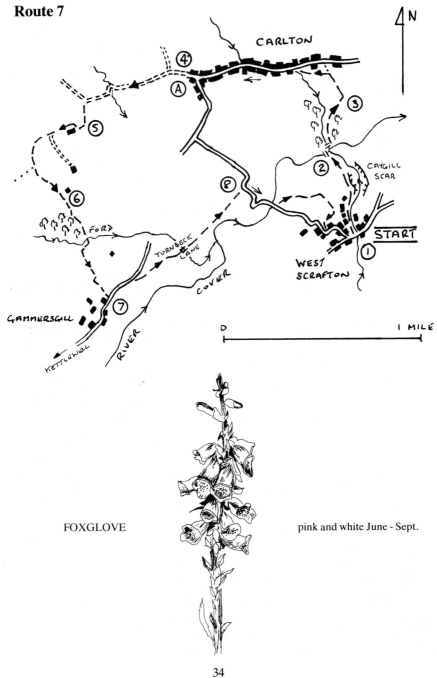

FOXGLOVE   pink and white June - Sept.

Route 7

Coverdale

4 miles
(shorter variation 2 miles)

START   *Bow Bridge in West Scrafton (G.R. NE074836), located on the Middleham to Kettlewell road. O.S. Outdoor Leisure Map 30 (Wensleydale sheet).*

ROUTE

1. *From east end of village cross Bow Bridge, turn right towards phone box and, with this on your left, proceed past Crag View cottage to footbridge. Cross this and continue up bank to fingerpost (**signed Lane End**). Turn right, descending again shortly to reach a stile. From here an obvious pathway leads down to Caygill Bridge.*

2. *Cross this and the bridge over Goodman Gill, through a gate and uphill along wall. After 40 yards, bear right to a signpost. Walk left then right by unusual alder with five trunks. Climb banking until a wall, then veer right, ignoring first gate on your left, to continue by fence to fingerpost in corner.*

3. *Go through gate and left up lane. After 100 yards, go left through gap stile and diagonally across next two pastures to a gate by barn. Turn right to road and left through village.*

4. *Where road forks take the right branch uphill to junction where bridleway joins. Keep left along tarmac road until this turns sharp right. Go straight forward through gate and walk diagonally left toward gate.*

5. *Go through gate, turn right and cross stile, walking right towards farm. Keep buildings on your left go through two gates, then left along track across a cattle grid. Ignore track left and continue on path to another gate. Go through this and along wall to a corner. Pass through broken wall and, turning left, go through first gate and turn right.*

6. *With barn on your left cross a stile in far wall and downhill with wood to your right. Ford Turn Beck and go up banking to wall. Turn right to corner. Go through gate. Keeping wall on your left (**yellow arrows**) reach a gate beneath mature ash. Turn left and follow field path to road.*

7. *Turn left to stile 60 yards later (**signed Carlton via Cover Lane**). Turn right then left across field to stile and here enter Turnbeck Lane. After ¼ mile go through gate and cross footbridge. Follow obvious footpath to the Gammersgill to West Scrafton road.*

8. *Turn right and cross Nathwaite Bridge. Walk uphill and turn left at gate* (**signed West Scrafton**), *then immediately through one on your right. Turn left along fence to cross a stile and go uphill to gate* (**fingerpost**). *Go through this and, still climbing, reach a fingerpost. Turn right between fence and wall and, keeping farm buildings on your left, continue forward. After third gate, walk uphill to a stile near a farm and turn left. Walk alongside building, through a gate, then turn left back into the village.*

SHORTER VARIATION
As for 1 to 4 then:

A. *Turn left down the road to cross Nathwaite bridge, then follow instructions from 8 onwards.*

ACCESS BY BUS
United Bus services from Richmond or Ripon.

———————

From Gammersgill, pleasant meadowland leads back to West Scrafton via the leafy delights of Turnbeck Lane, whose overgrown realm imparts to the walk a real expedition feeling for young children.

Refreshments   Foresters Arms, Carlton (outside tables).

WALDEN BECK, WEST BURTON

36

Bishopdale and Walden

Outline West Burton ~ Waterfall ~ Cote Bridge ~ Walden ~ Forelands Rigg ~ West Burton.

Summary Starting with a most delightful waterfall this route soon takes on the appearance of a steeple-chase due to the number of stiles that have to be crossed. The way traces good field paths however, heading up a tranquil but little known dale, known simply as Walden. Returning through a forest section, open ground at Forelands Rigg offers views across neighbouring Bishopdale on the approach back into West Burton.

Attractions West Burton is a picture-postcard village, with neat cottages forming the perimeter of a very large village green. Completing the rural scene are the stocks and an unusual market cross topped by a weather vane.

Just a couple of minutes from the foot of the village Walden Beck cascades over a fine waterfall into a wooded amphitheatre that is a very popular recreation spot in summer. Just downstream is a graceful arched bridge forming part of the route into the upper dale.

Pleasant pathways cut across rich meadowland flanking the course of Walden Beck, where several places offer scope for picnics and paddling, at Rookwith bridge for instance. At Riddings Farm the valley is spread at the walker's feet in all its splendour.

Down the east flank the deeply incised tributary of Thupton Gill divides the high fells of Pen Hill and Harland Hill. Climbing beside Thupton Gill a bridleway heads over the high ground for Coverdale.

Another bridleway heads up valley across the watershed into Wharfedale. Apart for these routes, there is no through road in Walden and most visitors would agree that the dale is better for it, having remained a peaceful backwater of the Dales. The valley head is presided over by Buckden Pike (702m) though on this walk it remains hidden from sight by a curve of the upper dale.

During the last Ice Age whilst glaciers swept down both upper Wharfedale and neighbouring Bishopdale gouging out the classical 'U' cross-sections, Walden meanwhile remained shielded from the ice movements by the bulk of Buckden Pike. Thus in Walden we see not only a beautiful valley, but one in appearance resembling what all pre-glacial valleys must have been like.

Some 2½ miles out of West Burton the walk turns back on itself and ascends through conifer forests ablaze with foxgloves in summer. Leaving

continued on page 40

Route 8

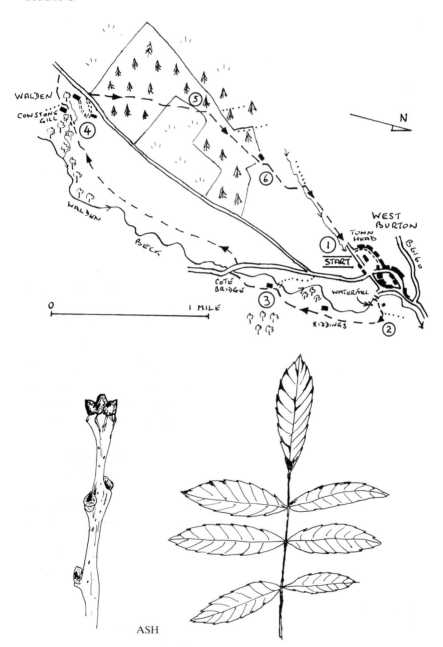

ASH

Route 8

Bishopdale and Walden   5 miles

START   *West Burton village, located just off the B6160 road along Bishopdale. (G.R. SE017866) O.S. Outdoor Leisure Map 30 (Wensleydale sheet). Parking around the village green.*

ROUTE

1. *At the lowest point of the village turn right and cross the bridge below the waterfall. Bear right, then left, climbing to a gate. Go through this, turning right towards a barn. Cross a stile and turn right along wall to a corner.*

2. *Bear right (signed **Rookwith and Cote Bridges**), then trace a field path (**look for paint spots**) to Rookwith Bridge.*

3. *Ignore bridge and bear left for Cote Bridge (**sign**) along a fence, then a wall to reach a gate. Enter lane and reach Cote Bridge after 150 yards. Turn right up the road, then left at a stile (**signed Cowstone Gill**). Follow the wall side for 80 yards and cross a second stile. For the next 1½ miles the obvious field path crosses many stiles (only 16 to go!).*

4. *After the 15th wall, head for the trees at the top right corner of the meadow. Cross the stile and descend to the footbridge.*

5. *Cross this and bear right through a gap stile, around the house and along a track leading to the dale road. Turn right and, after ¼ mile, cross a stile on the left into the woods (**signed West Burton and Newbiggin**). Go left, then right up a firebreak to a fingerpost. Take right-hand firebreak and, when the trees end, cross the ladder stile and head diagonally left to a stile and a gate.*

6. *Cross the stile and after ¼ mile a second one, turning right between a wall and fence. Cross stile after 200 yards and proceed down firebreak, through a gate to Forelands Farm.*

7. *Cross a track to a fence and cross stile here, aiming for a stile 200 yards distant among scattered trees. Cross this and, with a barn on your left, descend to a gap stile (**sign**) and then forward toward a ruined barn. Cross a stile and ford a small stream, then turn right (**signed West Burton**), following a path back into the village.*

ACCESS BY BUS
Nearest bus service. United Buses run a No. 26 bus to Hawes from Leyburn and Richmond, which calls at Aysgarth.

these at Foreland Rigg, views are enjoyed across Bishopdale toward Newbiggin and down towards Wensleydale at Aysgarth.

Refreshments The Fox and Hounds pub (outside table) and village store.

"SKELLDALE HOUSE" ASKRIGG

Askrigg and Mill Gill Force

Outline   Askrigg ~ Mill Gill Force ~ Helm ~ Whitfield Gill Force ~ Askrigg Beck ~ Askrigg.

Summary   A delightful short walk in Wensleydale, the largest of the dales and the home of course of the famous Wensleydale cheese. The start is in Askrigg where some sequences were shot for the T.V. vet. series All Creatures Great and Small. No problems will be experienced as all the walking is on easy field paths or lanes, rewarded with some fine waterfall scenery.

Attractions   Askrigg set in the beautiful Wensleydale, is the very epitome of Dales vernacular, a settlement with a long pedigree. It was mentioned in the Domesday Survey as Ascric. It forms a convenient starting point for a short but pleasant walk taking in wooded ravines and scenery for which the region is justly famed.

Wensleydale is at the true heart of Yoredale country, a term used to describe a geological sequence responsible for the terraced effect along the flanks of this and other northern dales. The rhythm or stepped effect in the strata seen along valley flanks has resulted in the profusion of waterfalls in the region, each full of character and beauty.

At the foot of the village main street just outside the church is where the walk begins. Across the street on the corner is the 18th century house that visitors familiar with the James Herriot series may recognise as one of the houses used for Siegfreid's surgery.

Askrigg was in fact one of the models used for Darrowby in the series and the Kings Arms, an old coaching inn just up the street a way, was the Drovers Arms. Askrigg was famous before the advent of television however when, Victorian sightseers took the train up the dale to visit the nearby waterfalls. The village once had a thriving industry in cheese making, mining and long-case clock manufacture.

From the church a short stroll leads quickly to a flagged field path to the old mill. From here a woodland trail in spring is covered with wood sorrel and anemones. Soon the sound of falling water can be heard and Mill Gill Force is reached where it plummets in two steps down a ravine. The return is effected via further cataracts, a green lane and field paths.

Refreshments   The Winville Hotel (children welcome).

Route 9

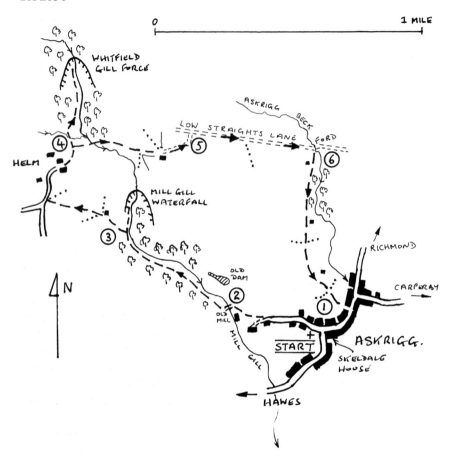

Route 9

Askrigg and Mill Gill   3 miles

START   *Askrigg (G.R. SD949910), situated on the minor road between Carperby and Bainbridge a mile from the latter. O.S. Outdoor Leisure Map 30 (Wensleydale sheet). There is space for a few cars outside the church.*

ROUTE

1. *Walk down the lane on the north side of the church as far as a gate at Mill Gill Cottage. Go through a stile on the right, following a paved path to a stile at the old Flax Mill. Cross stile and turn right to the stream.*

2. *Cross bridge and turn right, ignoring a stile on your left after about ¼ mile. Continue forward to Mill Gill Force after 200 yards. Return to and cross the stile.*

3. *Turn right, climbing alongside the wall, crossing a stile and walking forward to enter Skellgill Lane. Turn right into Helm and pick up a bridleway bearing right between the buildings.*

4. *After 200 yards leave the bridleway on a path diagonally across the pasture, crossing a small stream and a broken wall. Head for the far right corner of the next field by the trees. Cross a stile and continue through woods to waterfall. Return to the bridleway and turn east (left). Walk towards the wall corner, crossing a small stream and, with the farmhouse on your right, ascend to Low Straights Lane.*

5. *Turn right and, after nearly ¼ mile, reach a stile near a ford over Askrigg beck.*

6. *Turn right and, with woods over to your left, trace the obvious field path for ¼ mile downhill to a parting of the ways. Continue straight forward following the path quickly back into Askrigg.*

ACCESS BY BUS
United Buses service No. 26 from Leyburn and Richmond.

SEMERWATER

Route 10

Raydale and Semerwater

Outline   Countersett ~ Roman Road ~ Bainbridge ~ Roman Fort ~ River Bain ~ Semerwater ~ Carlow Stone ~ Countersett.

Summary   The discerning connoisseur of the countryside would be hard pressed to find a more picturesque corner of the county than Raydale. This bowerlike dale and the Bain, England's shortest river, enters Wensleydale at Bainbridge, an immaculate village with a pedigree stretching back at least as far as the Romans. Good paths and expansive views, a section of Roman military road, a fort, legends of a duelling giant and the devil, all add up to an interest-packed day out for all.

Attractions   Raydale seems hemmed in all around by high ground, imparting to the scene a sense of splendid isolation. Viewed from above the village of Countersett the eye is drawn in upon a view which unfolds majestically across and up Raydale. The jutting prow of Addleborough Hill (476m) overlooks the dale like the upturned hull of a wrecked ship.

Countersett itself consists of a handful of quaint cottages nestling peacefully in a fold of the hillside. The most interesting building here is undoubtedly Countersett Hall, a grade II listed building of considerable character.

There is a tradition, albeit unauthenticated, that King James I once stayed at the Hall. There are no such doubts about another important visitor however. George Fox, the founder of the Quaker movement, was a frequent visitor, sleeping in the small room above the entrance porch.

Raydale is probably a corruption of Roedale, derived one can assume, on account of the deer once flourishing in the long vanished Wensleydale Royal hunting forest. Bainbridge was a foresters' settlement and even today maintains a tradition linked with those distant times. At 9 p.m. each night from September 27th (Holy Rood) until Shrovetide the old forest horn is taken from the Rose and Crown, where it is kept, and sounded on the village green to guide any wayfarers abroad in the forest.

The eastern aspect of the village is dominated by Brough Hill where around 78 A.D. the Romans established the fortress of Virosidum. Little remains today of this outpost of the Roman war machine, yet the summit commands a fine prospect of the village and the surrounding dale.

Though peaceful looking enough, Semerwater is a lake of mystery and myth. The well known Ballad of Semerwater perhaps stems from the dawn of Christianity when the new faith was struggling to stem the tide of

continued on page 48

45

Route 10

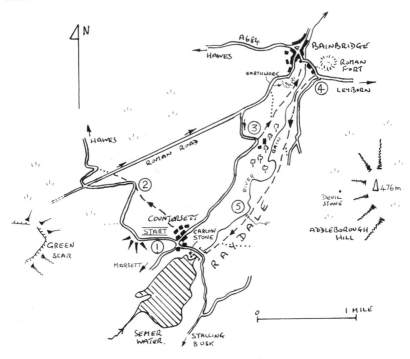

STOCKS, BAINBRIDGE

Route 10

Raydale and Semerwater

5½ miles

START *Countersett village, two miles south-west of Bainbridge on a
minor road from the latter to Marsett. (G.R. SD919878) O.S. Outdoor
Leisure Map 30 (Wensleydale sheet).*

ROUTE

1. *From the road junction walk towards Bainbridge. Turn left (***signed
Hawes End***) to reach a gate after 40 yards. Go through this and, with a
barn to your left, go through a gate. Cross a stream and go uphill,
keeping a second barn on your right, to reach a stile, and then ½ right to
the far wall. Turn right passing through a stile to enter a road.*

2. *Turn right and 100 yards later right again at a stile. (***signed Horton Gill
Bridge***). When the Roman road is met turn right, following this for 1¼
miles to a junction. Turn right to a bend after ¼ mile.*

3. *Turn left (***signed Gill Edge and Bainbridge***). 50 yards ahead go through
a gate and then left at a stile. Obvious field path descends toward woods,
crossing a tiny stream and, with a barn on your left, eventually traces the
edge of a ravine into Bainbridge by the Post Office. Turn right on A684
as far as the garage. To the left a path climbs to the Roman fort, however
continue up the road.*

4. *Just beyond garage turn right at a stile and along a path with the river
down to the right. At the top of Bracken Hill the path divides at twin
stiles. Cross the right-hand one and go downhill, across a stile to a gate
by a footbridge.*

5. *Cross the bridge and trace path through two stiles along the banks of the
river to Semerwater Bridge. Turn right and climb uphill into
Countersett village.*

ACCESS BY BUS
United Buses service No. 30 from Richmond and Darlington to Hawes
stops in Bainbridge.

paganism. The following rhyme was once taught to local school children . . .

> Semer Water rise, Semer Water sink.
> And swallow all the town, save this little house
> Where they gave me meat and drink.

According to tradition a fair town grew up alongside Raydale Beck. One winter day an old beggar wandered into town, penniless and hungry. He roamed in vain seeking food and shelter until he came upon the frugal dwelling of an aged couple too humble to be allowed a better position in the community. Taking pity on the traveller they fed him and gave him a bed for the night.

Taking his leave the next day he blessed the kind couple and turned to face the town that had rejected him. Uttering a curse, the content of which forms the children's ditty, the earth moved and the sky grew black pouring forth torrential rains. The tiny beck swelled until a large lake had formed swallowing the once proud town but not the old couple's cottage.

A second legend accounting for the lake relates how the Devil and a local giant fought each other from the summits of Wether Fell and Addleborough Hill, either side of Raydale. From their respective plinths the two adversaries hurled limestone boulders at each other, a distance of some six miles.

Two of the missiles, the Devil Stone and Carlow Stone, landed short of their intended mark. The former landed just below the summit of Addleborough, while the second, the Carlow Stone, fell in the valley bottom, seen today standing by the northern shore of Semerwater. Tradition has it that a third and much larger boulder formed such a colossal crater that it filled to create the present lake.

Refreshments The Rose and Crown (outside tables), Bainbridge. Children welcome.

Route 11

Langstrothdale and Stone Circle

Outline Hubberholme ~ Cray Gill ~ Cray ~ Scar House ~ Yockenthwaite ~ Stone Circle ~ Dales Way ~ Hubberholme.

Summary For this walk both long and short versions have much to commend them, guaranteed to hold the attention of children and parents alike. Always on good paths, well marked, a combination of riverside routes, waterfalls and a high-level traverse with distant views contrasts with history going back to the Bronze Age. There are any number of locations ideal for exploring, picnics, paddling and splashing about.

Attractions Upper Wharfedale is one of the finest of the Yorkshire Dales, especially that stretch above Buckden known as Langstrothdale. Bracken-covered flanks angle downwards to the shallow bed of the infant Wharfe, pierced here and there with rockmills. Everywhere limestone outcrops, whitened by the sun appear like the bleached bones of long dead dinosaurs. Whatever the season a visit to this beautiful valley is a must for the whole family.

The chosen starting point is Hubberholme, basically a pub, The George, and St. Michael's church. This was originally a forest chapel and was given to the monks of Coverham Abbey by William de Percy in 1241.

The structure is mainly 12th century and has a fine carved roof loft, one of the few to survive the decree of Elizabeth I that all such ornaments were to be destroyed. There is a 15th century font surmounting an older pedestal bearing pagan forms, as well as a plaque commemorating the fact that the Bradford-born playwright J. B. Priestley is interred nearby.

Much of the furniture, choir stalls, pews and chairs, were made by Robert Thompson, the famous 'mouseman' of Kilburn, whose trademark was a tiny carved mouse. Children will enjoy searching the building for these well-behaved church mice.

Leaving Hubberholme behind, a brief stroll on the lane leads to a pathway ascending beside the leafy delights of Cray Gill with its tiny packhorse bridge and numerous cascades. From Cray the route turns west and level going offers fine views of Buckden Pike and down the dale beyond Buckden.

Scar House was once a Quaker meeting place and was visited by George Fox. Here the shorter route turns off downhill.

continued on page 52

Route 11

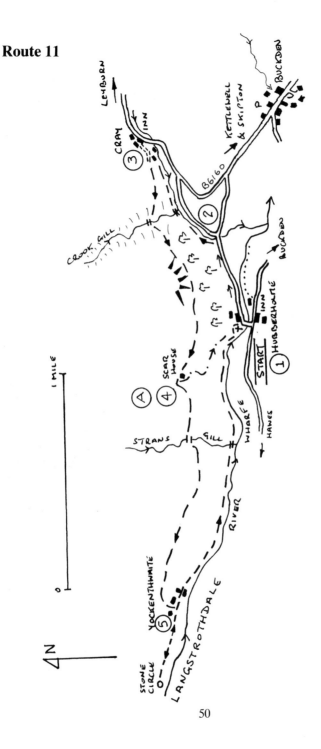

Route 11

Langstrothdale and Stone Circle

5½ miles

(shorter variation 2½ miles)

START   *Hubberholme (G.R. SD927782) O.S. Outdoor Leisure Map 30 (Wensleydale sheet). Hubberholme is easily reached by car from Skipton via the B6265 and B6160.*

ROUTE

1. *From the church walk down lane toward Cray as far as Stubbing Bridge.*

2. *Turn left (**signed Cray**), following path alongside stream, and cross ladder stile. Bear right here, soon crossing the bridge over Crook Gill (**care needed near edge of ravine in places**), then leaving beckside to climb toward Cray.*

3. *After passing house, and just before entering Cray, turn left along track to fingerpost (**Yockenthwaite and Scar House**) by gate. Go through this and continue on green track offering expansive views to Crook Gill. Cross footbridge and bear left, level going (**yellow paint spots**) for ¾ mile to Scar House.*

4. *Walk behind house to stile by gate. Cross this and forward through the odd rock outcrops, crossing footbridge over Strans Gill. Path continues with further stiles to a track. Turn down this into Yockenthwaite.*

5. *With farm on your left and a fingerpost ahead, a right turn through a gate beyond a barn follows a field path to stone circle. To continue, however, return to fingerpost and with farm on your left head downhill towards lower house and a gate (**signed Dalesway**). Go through gate and stile a few yards in front. Turn right immediately through second stile and follow riverside path, well marked, all the way back into Hubberholme.*

SHORTER VARIATION

As for 1 to 3 above, then:

A. *At Scar House turn left down stony track, following this downhill to enter Hubberholme by the church.*

ACCESS BY BUS

There are infrequent services (Keighley and District No. 72 from Skipton to Buckden. Pride of the Dales Buses, a new service to Cray and Hubberholme from Grassington starts Easter 1992.

The walk drops to river level at Yockenthwaite with its superb arched bridge. This was originally a Viking settlement, the place-name component -thwaite indicating a forest clearing; Yocken being a corruption of Eogon a personal name of Norse-Irish origin.

A short detour upstream from Yockenthwaite to see the Bronze Age stone ring precedes a return down the Dales Way long distance route back into Hubberholme, entering the hamlet from behind the church.

Refreshments The George Inn (beer garden), Hubberholme or White Lion (outside tables) in Cray.

CHURCH MOUSE, HUBBERHOLME

Buckden Pike and Roman Road

Outline   Buckden ~ Roman Road ~ Buckden Pike ~ Walden Road ~ Starbotton ~ River Wharfe ~ Buckden.

Summary   A great introduction to the high fell country of the Northern Dales, not unduly difficult but still demanding respect as the weather can deteriorate rapidly. The route takes advantage of Roman roads, green lanes, packhorse trails and the Dales Way riverside path. It is worth saving this walk for a clear day, for the view from the Pike (702m) extends as far as York Minster and the T.V. mast at Emley Moor!

Attractions   Upper Wharfedale, many would argue, is the finest of the Yorkshire Dales, and seen from the summit of Buckden Pike it would be hard to dispute this premise.

Above Kettlewell the dale displays that characteristic 'U' section typical of a glaciated valley. The floor since those times has gradually been levelled by the deposition of alluvial debris, jetsam of the swiftly flowing river.

Indeed the name Wharfe is said to originate from the Saxon guerf meaning swift. It certainly lives up to its name with cataracts like Mill Scar Lash, Ghaistrills Strid, Linton Falls and the infamous Strid.

Buckden village was originally a foresters' settlement, built on the edge of the great Langstrothdale Chase some time after the Domesday Survey, as evidenced by the fact that Starbotton was the last village up the dale to be recorded by the Normans.

Leaving Buckden the route to Buckden Pike follows the alignment of a Roman military highway, constructed in the first century A.D. under Agricola to link the fort of Virosidum (Bainbridge) with Olicana (Ilkley). There are still sections of the original surface to be seen in Rakes Wood.

Almost half a mile due south from the summit a cross stands in memory of a wartime bomber which crashed on the fell in January 1942. Only one of the five-man Polish crew survived, by crawling through the snow with a broken leg, following a fox's trail down into Buckden.

Back in the valley the route passes through Starbotton, once located on an important market road which crossed the dales from Settle to Masham. Looking at Starbotton today it is hard to imagine that it was once the scene of devastation. The village was practically wiped out by a tremendous flood which in 1686 tore down Cam Gill.

Linking Starbotton with Buckden, the Dales Way in parts traces the river along a picturesque path for two miles. There are plenty of places

continued on page 56

Route 12

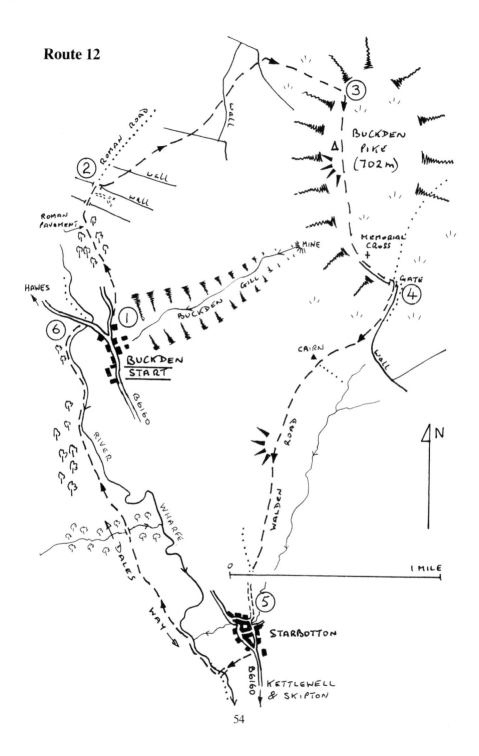

Roman Road

Wall

Wall

Wall

③

BUCKDEN PIKE (702 m)

△

②

Roman Pavement

MEMORIAL CROSS
+

GATE

MINE

BUCKDEN GILL

Hawes

①

BUCKDEN START

CAIRN

④

Wall

⑥

B6160

RIVER

WALDEN ROAD

N

WHARFE

DALES WAY

O   1 MILE

⑤

STARBOTTON

B6160

KETTLEWELL & SKIPTON

Route 12

Buckden Pike and Roman Road   7½ miles

START   *Buckden car park (G.R. SD942773) O.S. Outdoor Leisure Map 30 (Wensleydale sheet). Buckden is easily reached by way of B6265 and B6160 from Skipton, or A684 and B6160 from Northallerton.*

ROUTE

1. *Walk north out of the car park, through a gate and up a stony track through Rakes Wood. Note the Roman surface just before the road levels out. The bridleway levels out as a green track.*

2. *After the second gate veer right, tracing the bridleway over Cow Close for one mile before climbing steeply to the fell wall.*

3. *Turn right up the wallside following an obvious route to the triangulation pillar at the summit after a further ¼ mile. Continue along the boundary wall past the war memorial to reach a wall corner.*

4. *Turn right through a gate, following Walden Road, a bridleway enjoying superb views, for 2 miles down into Starbotton.*

5. *Walk through Starbotton and, at its south end, cross the dale road and continue on a walled pathway down to the river. Cross the bridge and turn right (Dales Way). Follow path up valley to Buckden Bridge after 2 miles.*

6. *Go through gap stile and turn right. Walk up road into village, turning left to the car park.*

ACCESS BY BUS

Keighley and District Buses, service 72 (infrequent) from Skipton. Pride of the Dales, a new bus service from Grassington to Buckden starting Easter 1992.

ideal for picnics on route and the chance to see dippers, kingfishers and herons.

Refreshments The Buck Inn, Buckden (tables outside). Fox and Hounds, Starbotton (tables outside).

LITTONDALE

Route 13   6 miles
Littondale and Wharfedale

Outline   Arncliffe ~ River Skirfare ~ Hawkswick ~ Knipe Scar ~ The Slit ~ Old Cote Moor ~ Cackle Rash Wood ~ Arncliffe.

Summary   A wonderful walk taking in three villages, one of them with T.V. and literary connections, and crossing high moorland offering extensive views. Well marked pathways should present no problems for the more experienced family group used to crossing open fells. Picturesque river sections and natural woodlands teeming with birdlife and flowers all add up to an interesting day out.

Attractions   The route begins in Arncliffe, a picturesque medieval village constructed about a large rectangular green. It takes its name from two Saxon words, earn (eagle) and clyf (cliff). The village was the original location used for filming Emmerdale Farm, The Falcon pub screened as the Woolpack.

Charles Kingsley visited the village and is believed to have written part of The Water Babies here, modelling his 'Vendale' on Littondale. Wordsworth too referred to the valley by its original name of Ammerdale.

Arncliffe's St. Oswald's church, built in the Perpendicular style, almost certainly stands upon the site of a Saxon wooden structure. It was rebuilt in 1793 and 1840, only the tower surviving from the 15th century. At that time the deceased of upper Wharfedale had to be carried over the high fells for burial at Arncliffe.

This was rather fraught especially in winter. In one documented instance a corpse was swept away by the raging waters of the Wharfe, and in another, eight bearers very nearly perished in deep snow on the 'tops'.

The Scandinavians who settled in the Littondale called its river skirr (clear) farr (bright stream) from which is derived the present name. From Arncliffe a pleasant path through meadows follows the riverside for two miles to Hawswick, above which may be seen traces of Anglian lynchets, or strip fields.

Where Wharfedale and Littondale merge just above Kilnsey, Old Cote Moor terminates in a rocky prow at Knipe Scar. In summer this forms a launching pad popular with hang gliders. Climbing up out of Hawkswick the path turns north at Knipe Scar before it descends through deciduous woods (hazel, haw, rowan, ash) to the Wharfe at Kettlewell.

continued on page 60

Route 13

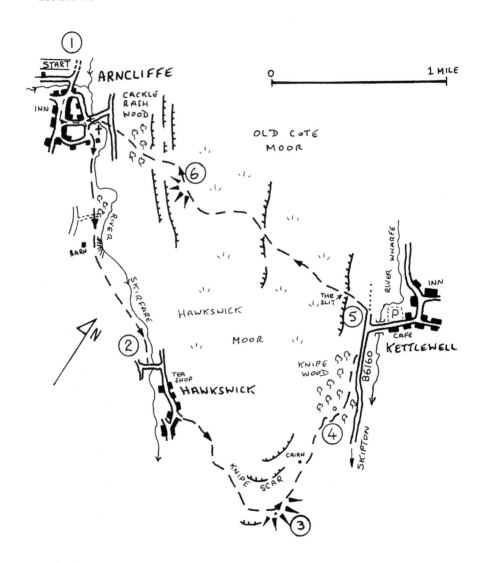

58

Route 13

Littondale and Wharfedale   6 miles

START   *In Arncliffe, parking at the north-western end of the village (G.R. SD930729) beside Darnbrook road. Village is reached by unclassified road from Skirfare Bridge on B6160. O.S. Outdoor Leisure Map 30 (Wensleydale sheet).*

ROUTE

1. *Cross arched bridge to south end of green. Turn left toward church, then right (**signed Hawkswick***) along what looks like a private drive. Bear left between garage and ruined barn and go through a gate. Head for riverbank and obvious path (**yellow paint spots***). After ½ mile cross two stiles and a narrow lane and head towards the river again. Go through a gate and, with a barn to your right, cross two stiles. Path skirts an eroded loop of the river then heads across wide pastures for ¾ mile.*

2. *Turn left at a stile and cross footbridge. Turn right into Hawkswick. When road divides, bear left up a track (**signed Kettlewell***). The path climbs steeply to the edge of Knipe Scar.*

3. *After bearing left at a cairn, the path levels out with good views of Great Whernside across the dale. By a larger cairn a rocky descent leads down to Knipe Wood.*

4. *Cross a stile and go through a gate. Pass through an enclosure, then, with a ruined building on your left, trace a woodland trail down to a gate. Go through this and turn left along road (**care***) to river bridge.*

5. *If needing refreshments cross bridge into village. Otherwise walk straight forward, ignoring a gate, to follow a stony track left to a second gate (**signposted Arncliffe***). Walk up wallside to fingerpost, then left uphill to a ladder stile. Cross this and aim for a nick (The Slit) in scarp. Scramble easily up this, then bear left (**yellow paint***) following clear path over the moors.*

6. *When the edge of Littondale is reached the path skirts the edge of rocky outcrops then descends through Cackle Rash Wood, a remnant of natural broad-leaf woodland. When road is reached cross to a stile. Go through this and trace riverside path toward church. Go through stile and turn left over bridge and forward to the village green.*

Cafes offers a chance to recuperate before climbing once again via The Slit for the open moor with fine views toward Pen-y-ghent. A descent through limestone scars at Cackle Rash Wood leads to a short riverside path back into Arncliffe.

Refreshments Tea room at Hawkswick. Choice of pubs and cafes in Kettlewell.

ICICLES IN DOWBERGILL

7½ miles
(shorter variation 4 miles)

Gt. Whernside

Outline Kettlewell ~ Dowbergill ~ Providence Pot ~ Hag Dike ~ Great Whernside ~ Tor Dyke ~ Cam Head ~ Kettlewell.

Summary The climb to Wharfedale's highest summit presents no great difficulties, these only arising on the next stage, across to Cam Head, should the mist come down. For this reason perhaps more experience should first be gained on other routes in this book. Part of the way is along the linear Tor Dyke, a defensive earthwork built around A.D. 70 by the Brigantes as a defence against the Romans.

Attractions Kettlewell is a picturesque village with many quaint stone-built cottages divided by a clear running brook. It was once a thriving mining community, lead having been won from a number of local mines, Providence being the more notable.

Following the brook upstream through the village eventually leads to a confluence, where Dowberbill joins from the west. Pleasant walking beside this stream leads past numerous cascades and old mine workings. It's a pretty valley with plenty of places suitable for picnics, safe for paddling and stick dipping.

A few yards before the stream divides again the entrance to Providence Pot is reached, located right in the middle of the beck. This was explored in the 1950s by cavers who discovered the notorious Dowbergill Passage. This runs straight as a die beneath the shoulder of Great Whernside, to emerge at Dow Cave a mile distant.

Above the cave entrance to the right spoil heaps indicate the whereabouts of Providence Mine. Just over the hill from Providence is Hag Dike, a remote farmhouse now serving as a Scout Field Centre. At this point anyone not wishing to continue to the top may return to Kettlewell along a green track back into the valley.

The summit of Great Whernside (704m) is a superb vantage point. The view extends several miles to the east across to Angram Reservoir in Nidderdale and beyond this to the western outliers of the North York Moors. It is one of the wildest tracks of upland countryside in England, the abode of grouse and curlew and beneath which cavers predict will perhaps be the second longest cave system in Europe.

Great Whernside takes its name from quernside, the hill where the querns or millstones came from. The summit continues north for ¼ mile,

continued on page 64

Route 14

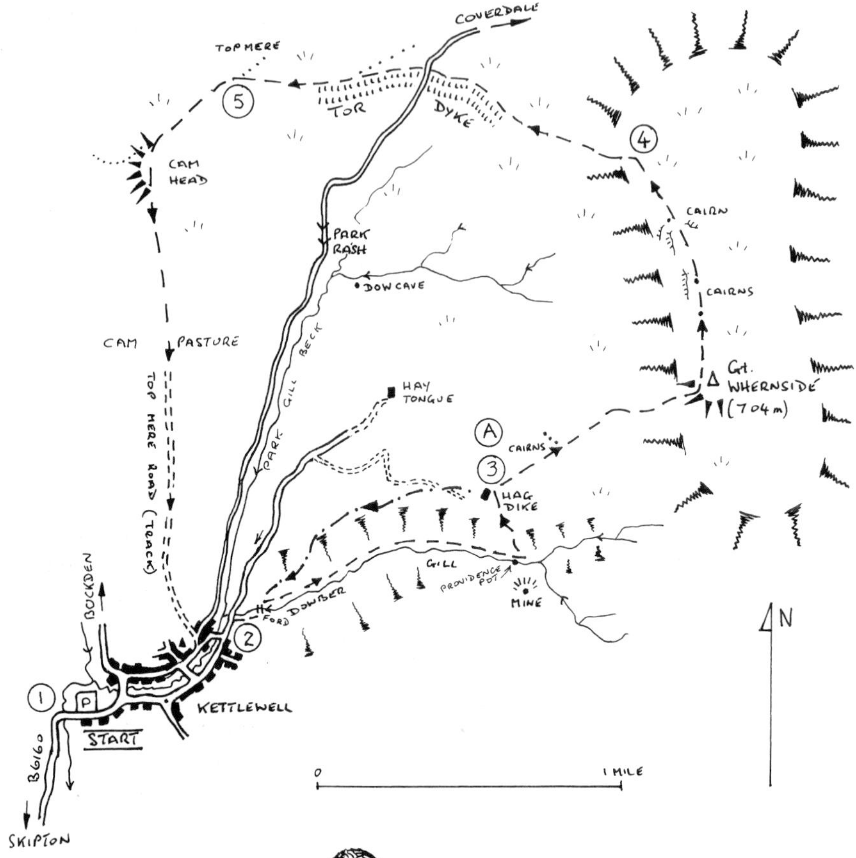
COVERDALE
TOP MERE
TOR
DYKE
CAM
HEAD
PARK
RASH
DOW CAVE
CAIRN
CAIRNS
CAM
PASTURE
TOP MERE ROAD (TRACK)
PARK GILL BECK
HAY
TONGUE
Gt.
WHERNSIDE
(704m)
CAIRNS
HAG
DIKE
GILL
PROVIDENCE POT
MINE
FORD
DOWBER
BUCKDEN
KETTLEWELL
START
B6160
SKIPTON
P
N
0
1 MILE

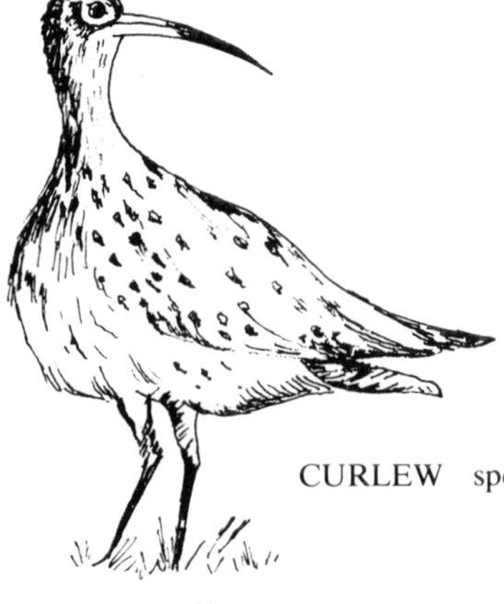

CURLEW speckled brown 54cm.

Route 14

Great Whernside

7½ miles
(shorter variation 4 miles)

START   *Kettlewell village, (G.R. SD968723), located on the B6160 five miles from Grassington. O.S. Outdoor Leisure Map 30 (Wensleydale sheet). Main car park beside river upon entering village.*

ROUTE

1. *Turn left out of car park and at the Smithy shop ignore bridge and go forward. At the maypole bear left to the Kings Head and straight forward with beck on your left as far as bridge.*

2. *Walk straight ahead on dirt track to where it crosses a small stream. Turn right beside this for a few yards to a ford and cross stream to gate. Go through this, turn right to ladder stile and follow Dowber Gill for about a mile. Just before beck divides beyond the capped entrance to Providence Pot, cross beck and walk steeply left up banking. The path levels out to Hag Dike.*

3. *Bear right in front of house and follow obvious path climbing east, passing some cairns and heading direct for the summit triangulation pillar amongst a pile of boulders. From the summit of Great Whernside walk north along broad ridge, a vague path passing two cairns, then descending by a third pile of stones to reach the wall corner.*

4. *Turn downhill beside wall and cross ladder stile on the right to follow path across boggy country to the road, walking roughly parallel with Tor Dyke over on your left. Cross road and continue on track, soon joining an old market road from the right. Follow Starbotton Road to Top Mere.*

5. *Another bridleway joins from your right, but continuing to Cam Head the path veers south on a two mile descent back into Kettlewell. At the tarmac road walk downhill, following road to the right and forward through village to return to start.*

SHORTER VARIATION   As for 1 to 2 above then:

A. *Pass through gate at Hag Dike and forward to gate. Go through this, bearing ½ left and forward through two wall gaps. Ignore track over on your right to cross a ladder stile. From here, clear track winds down the hillside to join the outward route just before ford.*

ACCESS BY BUS

Pride of the Dales running new bus service to Kettlewell starting Easter 1992.

then a path descends to a col at the head of Scale Park separating Great Whernside from its neighbour Buckden Pike. Across this pass the present motor road bisects Tor Dyke, a massive earthen bank erected around A.D. 74 by the Celtic hill tribes to defend the route across into Coverdale against the advancing Romans.

Refreshments The Kings Head pub (children welcome) and cafes in Kettlewell.

ST. MICHAEL'S, LINTON

Route 15

(shorter variation 4½ miles)

Grassington and the Snake Walk

Outline   Linton Falls ~ St. Michael's Church ~ Hebden ~ High Lane ~ Grassington ~ The Woggins ~ Ghaistrills Strid ~ Little Emily's Bridge ~ Linton Falls.

Summary   This route, for which there are two options, gives excellent value for the effort expended. It follows the river Wharfe for about half the course and includes falls and rapids as well as stepping stones for the adventurous. There is an ancient well, a packhorse bridge and curious ginnels in the centre of Grassington, the 'capital' of the upper dale. The walking is easy and diverse, full of interest for the whole family.

Attractions   Grassington originally began as a settlement at High Close, near Grass Wood, later growth being due to mining and textiles. There are many quaint cottages, shops and folk museum pressing in around its cobbled square; however behind this facade is a hotch-potch of ginnels, yards and alleyways with unusual sounding names - Lucy, Sam Pie Hill, Jakey and The Woggins.

The oldest building is the Old Hall, which dates from the 13th century. The bull-baiting stone can still be seen in the square midway between the old pump and the top tree.

Idyllic stretches of the beautiful Wharfe provide many a location for riverside picnics, safe paddling and bird watching with just a touch of history.

Beside the Wharfe is St. Michael's Church, a structure dating mostly from the 14th century. Some parts however, are much older, the bell tower for instance being 13th century. Inside can be seen a pre-reformation altar and a Jacobean pulpit.

Just downstream of the chapel a series of stepping stones give a river crossing to excite the children (adults too perhaps!). After this adventurous interlude a pleasant level stroll continues to Hebden. In summer the riverside banks and woods are ablaze with the blooms of vetch, king cups, monkey flower, sorrel, primrose, anemone and ragwort.

Hidden in Hebden Gill are traces of lead mining together with an ancient well. Though this is now being used as the water supply for a fish farm, Thruskell Well is believed to have originally been dedicated to the Norse god of thunder, Thor.

65

Route 15

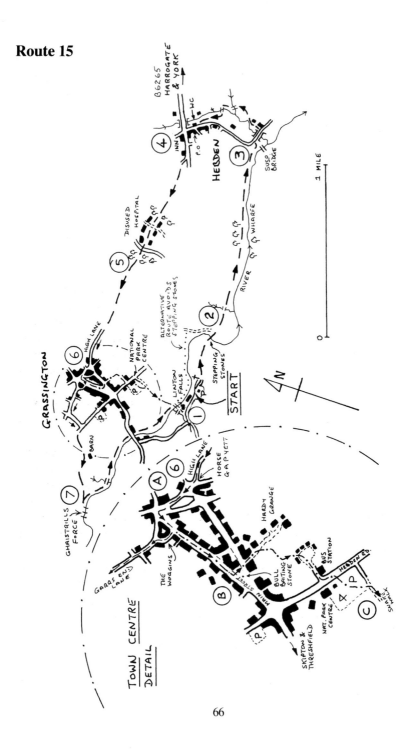

Route 15

Grassington and the Snake Walk

5½ miles

(shorter variation 4½ miles)

START   *Linton Falls, located just off the B6160 Burnsall to Threshfield road ¾ miles east of the latter. There is a car park provided (G.R. SE002632) O.S. Outdoor Leisure Map 30 (Wensleydale sheet) or Stile Maps (Grassington and District).*

ROUTE

1. *Turn right from the car park to reach the churchyard, and keeping to the right hand side, follow a footpath to a gate in corner. Go through and forward to the river.*

2. *Cross the stepping stones and up bank to a signpost. Go straight forward (**Burnsall**), following a riverside path for just over a mile.*

3. *At the suspension bridge turn left up wall side to gate (**fingerpost**). Turn right on Mill Lane and immediately after bridge (**signed Hebden and Bank Top**) turn left. Walk forward between houses on a path through pine trees to gate. Go through this and a second gate by some storage tanks. Veer left on track joining from right, then with fish farm on your right, cross two footbridges and go through a gate. Walk up hill with well (now a large pool) to your right to reach a wall. Go through a stile and up the bank. Ignore the bridge down to the right, tracing the fence to the road. Turn right into the village.*

4. *At the 'T' junction turn left, then right (**signed High Lane and Grassington**) up a green lane. When two gates are reached, cross a stile and turn left for the top corner of the field. Cross a stile, head across next pasture and over a stile. Crossing a farm track aim for a clump of pines, crossing another track. Go through the trees and head for the far end of the buildings to your right. Continue forward through trees and cross stile.*

5. *Walk forward with a barn on your left, to cross a stile. Well defined field paths then continue to High Lane. Follow this to Horse Gap Yett.*

6. *Turn right into the town, then left down Main Street. Just after the Dales Kitchen, turn right through alleyway (The Woggins) and left along Garrs End Lane. Taking the second left (Bull Ing Lane). Turn right after 20 yards, then left (**signed River Wharfe**). Go through a gate and head for a barn and gate. Go through this, walking around barn, then right at a wall corner. Veer ½ left to wall end by spring, go through gap stile and follow path to Ghaistrills Strid.*

67

7. *Walk downstream, following good path all the way back to road by bridge. Cross the road and go through a stile and continue on path to footbridge at Linton Falls. Cross river and trace path around to the right. At the steps a right turn leads to Little Emily's Bridge. Return to and climb the steps and turn left. Walk along the road back to the start.*

SHORTER VARIATION

As for 1 to 6 then:

A. *Walk right from Horse Gap Yett and turn left down Main Street.*

B. *Turn left outside Devonshire Hotel and continue ahead along Gills Fold. Pick up a path along wall side, following this to the right down into Springfield Road. Go past the bus station and at the 'T' junction turn left, then right into National Park car park. Head for far left corner.*

C. *Go through a gate and turn right down the flagged Snake Walk. Cross the footbridge and follow the path to the right, up some steps, then turn left. Walk along road back to start.*

ACCESS BY BUS

Keighley and District Buses service 72 from Skipton.

———————

Climbing out of Hebden gives views across to your left of the unique reef knolls. These are dome-shaped hills formed of especially pure limestones, deposited in much the same way as coral reefs, on the edge of a warm Carboniferous sea.

At Grassington it is decision time, to return down the Main Street and the Snake Walk (!) or to step through The Woggins, an ancient thoroughfare which predates the buildings now surrounding it, to emerge in Garrs End Lane on route for the river.

Quiet lanes lead gradually down to the Wharfe at Ghaistrills (ghostly rills) Strid. More waterside walking follows, with the river flowing in shallow shoals overhung by a wooded bank. Back at Linton Falls the quaint Little Emily's Bridge offers the chance for young children to feed the resident mallards.

Refreshments Clarendon Hotel (outside tables), Hebden. The Dales Kitchen tearoom, Cobblestones Cafe and numerous pubs in Grassington.

Route 16   8 miles

Nidderdale and How Stean Gorge

Outline   Scar House Reservoir ~ Dale Edge ~ Goyden Pot ~ How Stean Gorge ~ Middlesmoor ~ In Moor Lane ~ Scar House Reservoir.

Summary   This route is almost entirely on bridleways, obvious and clearly signed. It is low level in parts, following the normally dry stretches of the river Nidd past the entrance to the mysterious Goyden Pot. At the half-way point a refreshment halt provides the chance to explore the dramatic depths of the gorge at How Stean. On the whole the scenery is magnificent, sheer magic to the eyes. Allow a long summer day to enjoy this walk to its full.

Attractions   Nidderdale is an impressive valley in anyone's books, forming a steep sided trough which cuts a swathe across the wild tract of moorland that sweeps down from Great Whernside east towards Masham.

For reasons known only to those whose decision it was, Nidderdale was never included within the Dales National Park boundary, though it contains scenery every bit as dramatic and beautiful as other more celebrated spots.

From the car park by Scar House Reservoir a stroll across the wall of the old Bradford Corporation Works dam leads to a bridlepath winding up toward Woo Gill on the edge of Masham Moor. With a magnificent prospect of the upper reaches of the dale, the path bears east along Dale Edge, before descending to a leafy riverside route down the dale.

Just before reaching Limley Farm the entire river vanishes. A few yards beyond is Goyden Pot, its entrance lurking beneath a low shattered cliff in the far bank. Although the water next sees daylight at Nidds Head 1½ miles to the south, potholers have explored a 2 mile long labyrinth which includes a section of sporting riverway.

A pleasant stretch through meadowland leads to a short section of unavoidable road walking before cutting across field paths to Stean Beck. The shallow stream seen beneath the bridge gives no indication of the dramatic feature just a little way further upstream.

Walking up a narrow tarmac lane leads to a cafe where a track leads into a campsite. The bridge here spans the How Stean Gorge at its most impressive, a 50 feet deep canyon with sheer and overhanging walls.

Refreshments may be taken here before going on to explore the gorge (there is a charge). The gorge is deeply undercut at some points,

continued on page 72

Route 16

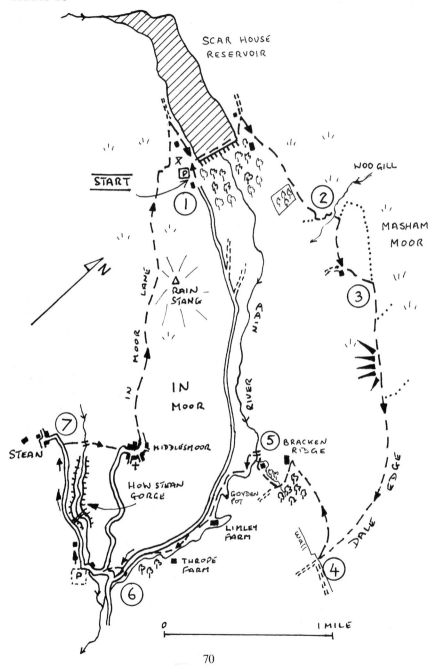

SCAR HOUSE
RESERVOIR

WOO GILL

START

MASHAM
MOOR

N

RAIN
STANG

IN
MOOR

MOOR LANE

RIVER NIDD

⑤ BRACKEN
RIDGE

⑦

STEAN

MIDDLESMOOR

HOW STEAN
GORGE

GOYDEN
POT

LIMLEY
FARM

THROPE
FARM

WALL

DALE EDGE

④

⑥

0   1 MILE

Route 16

Nidderdale and How Stean Gorge   8 miles

START   *The car park and picnic area at Scar House Reservoir (G.R. SE069766) O.S. Outdoor Leisure Map 30 (Wensleydale sheet). The car park is reached by the Yorkshire Water Authority toll road from Lofthouse.*

ROUTE

1. *Walk towards dam, going through gate and turning right along dam walkway. At the far end turn left up track then right (**signed Nidderdale Way**). A clear path climbs to top edge of wood, contouring along hill to gate. Go through this and descend to Woo Gill.*

2. *Cross gill and next small stream. Ignore bridleway climbing to the left and follow obvious way contouring to the right to reach a gate by hut. Go through this and turn ½ left, uphill to meet bridleway.*

3. *Turn right with level going for almost 2 miles with square wood seen in distance. Eventually at Dale Edge a gate is reached at a wall corner.*

4. *Ignore gate by turning downhill to your right, passing through a wall, and with wood on your left reach farm. Turn left along bottom of wood, following track to gate. Go through this and after crossing a stream turn right, descending beside tree to a barn. Bear right below barn to stile. Cross and continue along riverbank to stile 50 yards ahead.*

5. *Cross stile and footbridge, then turn left along obvious footpath tracing river. After Goyden Pot turn right in Limley Farm yard. When track turns sharp right, go forward through gate (**Nidderdale Way**).*
   Ignore path crossing river to aim for stand of pines ahead, eventually meeting road. Turn left and when pines end leave road at first stile on left. Bear ½ right to Thrope Farm, making for point between barn and river. There is no stile provided, so cross wall with care and turn right along track. Turn left at first gate, cross pasture to riverside and follow this back to road after ¼ mile. Turn left towards Lofthouse.

6. *Just after Water Auth. Ticket kiosk turn right on footpath (**signed Middlesmoor**). Veer right behind barn to enter road. Walk forward along lane (**signed How Stean**) and follow this uphill to the cafe. After viewing gorge continue up road toward Stean.*

7. *Just before village turn right (**signed Middlesmoor**). Obvious path descends to bridge over gorge, then climbs to road. Turn left uphill and follow road through village, and continuing via In Moor Lane. After 2 miles this winds down to track by Scar House Reservoir. Turn right and return to car.*

providing an adrenalin stimulating route for visitors. Here the path spans the depths on sweeping bridges, there clinging impressively to the lichen-streaked limestone.

Leaving How Stean the route climbs steeply up through the village of Middlesmoor, then takes a moorland lane across Rain Stang back to the start at the reservoir.

Refreshments How Stean cafe (children's play area). Also the Crown Hotel (outside tables) in Middlesmoor.

STANDING STONE   Route 6

Appendices

ROUTES IN ORDER OF DIFFICULTY

The walks are arranged into four categories according to distance, and within each category they are listed in order of difficulty. This is assessed on the basis of how strenuous the walks are relative to other routes in the same category.

Easy Walks (up to 4 miles)
Route 2 — *Kisdon Gorge and Muker (variation)* — *2 miles*
Route 9 — *Askrigg and Mill Gill Force* — *3 miles*
Route 11 — *Langstrothdale and Stone Circle (variation)* — *2½ miles*
Route 7 — *Coverdale (variation)* — *2 miles*
Route 1 — *Five Dales Walk (variation)* — *3½ miles*
Route 5 — *Arkengarthdale (variation)* — *3¾ miles*

More strenuous walks (up to 5 miles)
Route 8 — *Bishopdale and Walden* — *5 miles*
Route 14 — *Gt. Whernside (variation)* — *4 miles*
Route 4 — *Reeth and the Maiden Castle* — *4½ miles*
Route 3 — *Hard Level Gill* — *5 miles*
Route 2 — *Kisdon Gorge and Muker* — *5 miles*
Route 7 — *Coverdale* — *4 miles*
Route 15 — *Grassington and the Snake Walk (variation)* — *4½ miles*

Easy longer walks *(5 miles or more)*
Route 13 — *Littondale and Wharfedale* — *6 miles*
Route 10 — *Raydale and Semerwater* — *5½ miles*
Route 6 — *Middleham and Coverham Abbey (variation)* — *5¾ miles*
Route 6 — *Middleham and Coverham Abbey* — *6½ miles*
Route 11 — *Langstrothdale and Stone Circle* — *5½ miles*

Strenuous walks *(5 miles or more)*
Route 16 — *Nidderdale and How Stean Gorge* — *8 miles*
Route 5 — *Arkengarthdale* — *7¼ miles*
Route 1 — *Five Dales Walk* — *7 miles*
Route 14 — *Gt. Whernside* — *7½ miles*
Route 12 — *Buckden Pike and Roman Road* — *7½ miles*
Route 15 — *Grassington and the Snake Walk* — *5½ miles*

BUS OPERATORS RELEVANT TO THE WALKS:

Pennine Buses .... Tel. (0756) 749215
United Buses .... Tel. (0325) 468771
Pride of the Dales .... Tel. (0756) 753123

RAILWAY INFORMATION:
British Rail enquiries. Tel. Leeds (0532) 448133
Skipton (0756) 792543
Carlisle (0228) 44711

NATURE RESERVES/TRAILS:
Harlow Carr Botanical Gardens, Harrogate.
Grass Wood.

WET WEATHER ALTERNATIVES:
Masham Brewery Visitor Centre. (appointment only). Tel. (0756) 89057 ext. 4317.

MUSEUMS AND HISTORIC BUILDINGS:
Richmond Castle. Tel. (0748) 2493.
Middleham Castle. Tel. (0969) 23899.
Fountains Abbey and Studley Royal. Tel. (076586) 333.
Castle Bolton. Tel. (0969) 23981.
Yorkshire Carriage Museum, Aysgarth. Tel. (0969) 663652.
Upper Wharfedale Folk Museum, Grassington. Tel. (0756) 752800.
Swaledale Folk Museum, Reeth. Tel. (0748) 84517.
The Watermill Inn, Pately Bridge. Tel. (0423) 711484.
Green Howards Regimental Museum, Richmond. Tel. (0748) 2133.
Low Mill, Bainbridge. Tel. (0969) 50416.
Dales Countryside Museum, Hawes. Tel. (0969) 667450.
Richmondshire Museum, Richmond. Tel. (0748) 5611.
Nidderdale Museum, Pately Bridge. Tel. (0423) 711225.
Crakehall Water Mill, Bedale. Tel. (0677) 23240.
Bolton Priory. Tel. (075671) 238.
Ripley Castle. Tel. (0423) 770152.
Pump Room Museum, Harrogate.
Constable Burton Hall, Leyburn. Tel. (0677) 50428.
Kiplin Hall and Grounds, Scorton, Nr. Richmond. Tel. (0748) 818178.
Ripon Cathedral.
Newby Hall and Gardens, Ripon. Tel. (0423) 322583.
Parcival Hall and Gardens, Appletreewick.

Pony Trekking and Riding:
Kilnsey Trekking Centre, Wharfedale. Tel. (0756) 752861.
New Close Farm, Gammersgill, Coverdale. Tel. (0969) 40668.
Swaledale Trekking Centre, Reeth. Tel. (0748) 84581.

Show Caves:
Stump Cross Caves, Greenhow. Gift shop and cafe. Tel. (0423) 711042.
Mother Shipton's Cave and the petrifying Dropping Well Knaresborough. Tel. (0423) 864600.

National Park Visitor Centres:
Hawes Tel. (09697) 450.
Grassington. Tel. (0756) 752748.
Aysgarth Falls. Tel. (09693) 424.

Steam Railway:
Yorkshire Dales Railway, Embsay. Tel. (0756) 794727.
Darlington Railway Centre/Museum. Tel. (0325) 460532.

Craft Centres and Galleries:
Moorside Design Ceramic, West Burton.
Old School Arts Workshop, Middleham. Tel. (0969) 23056.
Jig A Jogs Toys (traditional and hand-painted). Tel. (0969) 667008.
Bishopdale Forge. Tel. (0969) 478.
Small World (dolls houses and miniatures), Aysgarth. Tel. (0969) 663723.
Ivor Grace (wood turner), Askrigg. Tel. (0969) 50663.

Greystone Studio, Gunnerside. Tel. (0748) 86363.
Logan Gallery, Pletts Barn, Grassington. Tel. (0756) 753043.
Uredale Glass, Masham. (Ripon) 89780.
The Hawes Ropemaker. Tel. (0969) 667487.
Mews Crafts, Reeth.
The Pot Shop, pottery, Reeth.
Reeth Gallery, art.
The Pottery Emporium, Aysgarth.
West Witton Pottery. Tel. (0969) 22755.

OTHER PLACES OF INTEREST:

Brimham Rocks, Pately Bridge. (NGR SE210650).
Yorke's Folly, Glasshouses. (NGR SE158636).
Easby Abbey.
Ellerton Priory (NGR SE080974).
Barden Tower (NGR SE051571).
Druid's Temple (folly). Nr. Masham. (NGR SE175787).
Coverham Abbey. (NGR SE106864).
Jervaulx Abbey. (NGR SE172857).
Marrick Priory. (NGR SE067978).
Maiden Castle, Swaledale. (NGR SE022981).
Yockenthwaite Stone Circle. (NGR SD899794).
Roman Road, Buckden Raike. (NGR SD939782).
Ta Dyke, Iron Age Earthwork. (NGR SD985985).
Hubberholme Church. (NGR SD926783).
Old Gang Mining ruins. (NGR NY975005).
Arncliffe village, Emmerdale farm location, also where Charles Kingsley wrote much of The Water Babies.
Virosidum Roman Fort, Bainbridge. (NGR SD937901).
High Close, Grassington. Romano-Celtic field systems. (NGR SE005655).
Lea Green, Romano Celtic enclosures. (NGR SD997664).
Thorpe Perrow Arboretum, Bedale. Tel. (0677) 22480.
Lady Well, Threshfield, ancient well with associated legends. (NGR SD998636).

TOURIST INFORMATION:

Bedale. Tel. (0677) 24604.
Leyburn. Tel. (0969) 23069.
Richmond. Tel. (0748) 850252.
Kirkby Stephen. Tel. (07683) 71199.
Brimham Rocks. Tel. (0423) 780688.
Pately Bridge. Tel. (0423) 711147.
Reeth. Tel. (0748) 84517.
Grassington. Tel. (0756) 753083.

Swimming Pools/Leisure Centres:

Long Ashes, Threshfield. Tel. (0756) 752261.
Richmond. Tel. (0748) 4581.
Nidderdale Sports Centre, Patley Bridge. Tel. (0423) 711442.

Leisure Parks:
    Kilnsey Park, fish farm. Tel. (0756) 752150.
    Blackburn Trout Farm, Gayle. Tel. (0969) 667524.
    Lightwater Valley, Ripon. Tel. (0765) 85321.

MARKET DAYS:

Hawes	Tuesday
Leyburn	Friday
Richmond	Saturday
Kirkby Stephen	Monday
Ripon	Thursday
Masham	Wednesday

PERSONAL SAFETY ON THE HILLS

It cannot be stressed enough that ramblers should go prepared for all eventualities. Pennine weather can change suddenly and be a complete contrast between the valleys and high fellsides. If crossing exposed moorland or high ground always:

Wear appropriate footwear and carry suitable waterproofs.

Carry map and compass and have the knowledge of how to use them.

Carry a torch, whistle and spare food.

Never walk alone and always leave details for your route.

Take extra caution with children near deep water.

Never enter caves or approach the brink of shafts. Any interest in caving should be developed through one of the recognised caving clubs for the area.

In the event of an emergency never leave an injured person alone. If injuries allow it, move to a sheltered position safe from additional hazards, water, loose boulders or cliff edge. If unconscious leave in a position where vomiting is unlikely to cause choking.

Cover the injured party with spare clothing, or better still, place in an exposure bag. Remember the universally recognized distress signal is six long blasts on a whistle or flashes with a lamp, repeated at one minute intervals.

To summon help dial 999 or Settle police and ask for Fell Rescue.

YOCKENTHWAITE CIRCLE   Route 11

FAMILY WALKS SERIES

Family Walks in the North Yorkshire Dales. Howard Beck. ISBN 0 907758 52 5.

Family Walks in West Yorkshire. Howard Beck. ISBN 0 907758 43 6.

Family Walks in Three Peaks and Malham. Howard Beck. ISBN 0 907758 42 8.

Family Walks in South Yorkshire. Norman Taylor. ISBN 0 907758 25 8.

Family Walks in the North Wales Borderlands. Gordon Emery. ISBN 0 907758 50 9.

Family Walks in Cheshire. Chris Buckland. ISBN 0 907758 29 0.

Family Walks in the Staffordshire Peak and Potteries. Les Lumsdon. ISBN 0 907758 34 7.

Family Walks in the White Peak. Norman Taylor. ISBN 0.907758 09 6.

Family Walks in the Dark Peak. Norman Taylor. ISBN 0 907758 16 9.

Family Walks in Snowdonia. Laurence Main. ISBN 0 907758 32 0.

Family Walks in Mid Wales. Laurence Main. ISBN 0 907758 27 4.

Family Walks in South Shropshire. Marian Newton. ISBN 0 907758 30 4.

Family Walks in the Teme Valley. Camilla Harrison. ISBN 0 907758 45 2.

Family Walks in Hereford and Worcester. Gordon Ottewell. ISBN 0 907758 20 7.

Family Walks around Cardiff and the Valleys. Gordon Hindess. ISBN 0 907758 54 1.

Family Walks in the Wye Valley. Heather and Jon Hurley. ISBN 0 907758 26 6.

Family Walks in Warwickshire. Geoff Allen. ISBN 0 907758 53 3.

Family Walks around Stratford and Banbury. Gordon Ottewell. ISBN 0 907758 49 5.

Family Walks in the Cotswolds. Gordon Ottewell. ISBN 0 907758 15 0.

Family Walks in South Gloucestershire. Gordon Ottewell. ISBN 0 907758 33 9.

Family Walks in Oxfordshire. Laurence Main. ISBN 0 907758 38 X.

Family Walks around Bristol, Bath and the Mendips. Nigel Vile. ISBN 0 907758 19 3.

Family Walks in Wiltshire. Nigel Vile. ISBN 0 907758 21 5.

Family Walks in Berkshire and North Hampshire. Kathy Sharp. ISBN 0 907758 37 1.

Family Walks on Exmoor and the Quantocks. John Caswell. ISBN 0 907758 46 0.

Family Walks in Mendip, Avalon and Sedgemoor. Nigel Vile. ISBN 0 907758 41 X.

Family Walks in Cornwall. John Caswell. ISBN 0 907758 55 X.

Family Walks on the Isle of Wight. Laurence Main. ISBN 0 907758 56 8.

Family Walks in North West Kent. Clive Cutter. ISBN 0 907758 36 3.

Family Walks in the Weald of Kent and Sussex. Clive and Sally Cutter. ISBN 0 907758 51 7.

Family Walks in the North Yorkshire Dales. Howard Beck. ISBN 0 907758 52 5.

The Publishers, D. J. Mitchell and E. G. Power welcome suggestions for further titles in this Series; and will be pleased to consider manuscripts relating to Derbyshire from new or established authors.